DARE TO BE A
DIFFERENCE
Maker
Volume 6

DARE TO BE A

DIFFERENCE
Maker
Volume 6

DIFFERENCE MAKERS WHO DARE TO LIVE
WITH PASSION, FOLLOW THEIR PURPOSE
AND COMMIT TO HELPING OTHERS!

MICHELLE PRINCE

Dedication

To all the "Difference Makers" in the world
who are making a difference by following your heart.
Thanks for letting your "light" shine!

Introduction

For many years as I worked in "Corporate America" I would say to myself, "I just want to make a difference!" I was selling software and I'm sure I was making some difference for my clients but not in the way I wanted to. I wanted to help, serve, encourage and motivate people. I wanted to make a positive impact on their lives but I didn't know how…how could just one person really make a significant difference? So I didn't…for a long time. I continued to work in an area that wasn't my passion or calling. I didn't follow my heart and God's promptings to go in the direction of my purpose and dreams. Instead, I just let year after year go by feeling unfulfilled, unhappy, and spiritually broken.

That is, until one day in 2008 when I had my "aha" moment. It hit me like a ton of bricks that it's my responsibility to follow my passions and purpose. No one can do that for me. I took action to write my first book, *Winning In Life Now*, began to speak, motivate and mentor others to live their best life and, as they say, "the rest is history."

What I found over this journey is that we all have a desire to make a difference. We all want to live with passion and follow our God-given callings; our purpose. It's through this understanding that I decided to write this series of books.

Dare To Be A Difference Maker 6 is my vision to have a unique collection of narratives, not only from inspired leaders, but also from those I see making a difference and impacting others in their everyday personal and professional life. These stories are about *real* people who are making a *real* difference, even on a small scale.

My mission in creating the "Difference Maker Movement" and in writing the series of *Dare To Be A Difference Maker* books is that you will gain inspiration, wisdom, and the courage you need in order to get through life's tough challenges and make a difference for others in the process.

So many people I speak with these days discuss their issues as though they are losing hope. It is my vision for this book to reach the masses and have a powerful effect on people in their everyday lives. It is my prayer that this book, and all the volumes, will breathe new life into your mind and spirit and that it will inspire you to take action in order to help others.

I've selected an exclusive group of difference-makers who I know can motivate, inspire, and be a part of a movement to change people's lives. Everyone can do this; it just takes commitment and honoring of our unique and sacred gifts. It is to those people I dedicate this book.

From one "Difference Maker" to another,

Michelle

P.S. Do you or anyone you know have a story about making a difference? We are currently interviewing authors for our next book and would love to have you join us in this amazing journey. To submit an entry, please contact Info@PrincePerformance.com for more details. While one powerful story can be fascinating many can move mountains!

Table of Contents

1

Open For Him

Heather Anderson

We all have a story planted deep in our souls, full of emotion, tribulation and triumph. They are more than a journey, consisting of smooth sand, pebbly rocks, and winding paths in steep mountains. The path I have been called to travel is God's. I delight in sharing how God has taken me off "Heather's Highway" and as I surrendered, blessed me with the most beautifully wrapped present by His Heavenly Angels! His gift transformed the deepest core of my heart. Inside is our story, my calling is to become His writer, to create "God's Messenger's, and spot his radiant hearts.

If someone were to ask me the question, "When was my faith" branded" on my heart"? My simple answer would be no other than, "At birth!" But it grew with my parent's unconditional love and God's Love, as they each gifted me with this daily branding, called faith. However, it didn't move mountains until in my early 30's when my knees hit the floor, and I found myself at the foot of His Robe! It was in those open moments for Him, when I felt the corner of His Robe brush gently against my cheek, wiping my tears when my faith Rose to His Calling for me.

My story started long before kneeling in prayer, but "Our Story", started the moment I rose from my knees in prayer. As God blessed me over the years with exactly what my heart desired, like being the Mary Poppins

I always dreamed of, and working with many of His beautiful children, He also blessed me with one of my biggest blessings, my beloved husband, Andy. Andy and I were high school sweethearts! Ah yes, that sounds cute, but we had many hurdles to cross, faith being one of them. We were born into different denominations and it took 12 years, many break ups, and AMAZING moments which led us to God's Altar! We put God first, in all that we did. And although it was a long journey, we have been blessed with marital bliss! Praise God we are living proof that different church upbringings did not hinder our marriage. With faith becoming our number one priority, God blessed our hands and hearts in marriage. We have helped hold each other accountable with faith many times throughout the years. (May I repeat, MANY times) As God continued to bless us in His mighty ways in our marriage, He also blessed us in mightier ways with our three beautiful children, Chloe, Breck and Keegan! Life couldn't get richer than raising our three angels together in God's Salt and Light!

With a righteous faith stronger than one could imagine, Andy conquered his role of being our sole provider so selflessly. I was blessed to be the stay at home Mom I had always dreamed of being! We thanked God daily for our family's blessings. However, this gifted path did bring many financial bumps our way. With each hardship, we clutched to our faith and thanked God in humble amazement as HE has always provided for our family. How merciful, how great and how amazing our God is!!! He not only held Andy up during his time of juggling 4 jobs at once, He blessed us beyond our wildest dreams. In times of doubt, tears and fear, He provided for our family, just as HE does daily for ALL of His families!!

With those blessings comes hardships at times, and I can vividly remember one particular night I completely and totally had what one may call "a breaking point". After one of the roughest rides we were called to juggle financially, I took Andy face to face one night after we tucked the kids in bed, and whole heartedly said, "Andy, I love you and thank you from the bottom of my heart for working SO many jobs for our family, but why does it have to be so hard for us? There's got to be an easier way. You provide for us in so many remarkable, selfless ways more than any amount of money could provide for us. Can you talk to your boss? Can I tell him and show him how hard you are working and deserving of more? I'm praying for you, Andy, every day and maybe we need to pray on finding you a new job?"What rolled out of his mouth next was so immediate, that I can vividly remember it as if it was yesterday. In fact, it was actually 5 years ago and Andy and God said together so beautifully in unison, "Heather, I really appreciate your prayers, but I think you need to pray for yourself."I was left speechless, which led to pure transformation. Just hours after Andy spoke those words to me, I found myself on our hallway floor, on my hands and knees, in the middle of the night, in the dark, just God and me. That night was the first time in seven years that I discovered this was one of the best places to pray in our home! Just as quick as my knees hit the floor, I found myself thanking God for letting me use the corner of His Robe to dry my tears, and then I found myself boldly and bravely saying, "I surrender to you God! 100% I surrender to you God. I thought I was already doing what you wanted as a full time stay at home Mom, nursery teacher, and community volunteer, but I surrender my all to you right now! Please take me where you want me to go if it involves more than what is already on my plate". AT THAT MOMENT IN MY RISE FROM KNEELING, I was left behind as HE ROSE ME IN HIS CALLING.

God picked me up, in my sleep, in the dead of night and guided me on a new journey. He set me down at our computer, my every word written became His spoken. His hand typed my every letter on the keyboard, as it came from the deepest depths of His Heart. It flowed so quick and so freely, that our writing together easily filled 4 pages within 20 minutes!!! I remember looking up at Him in heaven at times saying, "God really me? Do you see these run on sentences? Do you remember my math background?"Not only did I need grammar correction, I looked like a hot mess at times when He called me to write in the wee early morning hours with frazzled hair and Starbucks coffee cups taking up my entire office desk! I also may have looked out of sorts when I grabbed a napkin at Happy Donuts one Saturday morning with my family, only to write frantically fast out of the blue! Ha, sometimes we just need to laugh at ourselves in life when we surrender!

All the while, He had a plan and was molding me into His Calling. I went, and listened, and obeyed, and developed a burning love for our Christian writing journey together! You see at first when He took my hand in writing, I didn't follow the book "Writing for Dummies" correctly. My reason, I NEVER READ IT!!! I NEVER took a writing class in my life! On many of our "writing" days, my home looked nothing like the HGTV show I so desired. Our home became decorated with laundry, toys, and dishes our youngest was running right through in his cute diapers with his cars and trains gliding over the mess. But it was a beautiful mess I must say! Even in the calm and chaos, every ounce of my soul longed to be guided by Him. My heart was on fire for every word He spoke to me as we wrote together. In fact, many times after His Grandest writings, our office doors would fling open and I would find myself running around our house shouting, "I'm on FIRE! I'm on FIRE!"! Anyone peeking through our window would have thought I was absolutely crazy! I desired nothing greater than to share His homework from above with ALL of His people!!

Being on fire for God set my heart on such a journey that I bought a "promise ring for God". I promised that I would wear it daily until I published His work. This ring bonded my commitment and promise to Him to write when He called. I remember reminding myself at times, working for God doesn't always involve order or perfection, like I sometimes desired, but His Love He delivered to my heart in this calling kept me at His feet in perseverance and such thankfulness and divine gratitude, that my heart was forever grateful. It was a powerful-led journey that had such an impact on me from the beginning that I have not read a book except children's books and the Bible, since day one of our writing journey, 5 years ago! (Once again it may have looked crazy as I would bee line through Barnes and Noble to reach story time with Keegan as not to get distracted or influenced by other's writings.) I knew without a doubt that this journey He called me on was all Him and me. His delivery of His work in my heart and hands has been that of a straight arrow connecting us both together from heaven to earth, leaving no path for any distractions, but making all the room in the world to share His words with all!

This next delivery began one evening in a restaurant when my Mom and I were eating dinner together. My attention was directed toward a long table filled with laughter, red boas and hats. It was none other than one amazing Red Hats Group! I yearned to know more about this group. The entire drive home I couldn't wait to find out how quickly we could join, and learn what they were all about. After I Googled this group, my enthusiasm for joining immediately came to a complete screeching halt after I read their age requirement of membership. Rats! I had to wait 20 years before I could join. But when one door shuts, another opens. SO the idea of starting a group, BUT making a difference in so many lives started to burn through every hair on my body! That night, I tucked our oldest daughter into bed with my heart stirring. It was in those nighttime hours when the spark of inspiration hit my soul deeper that I had ever imagined! I just kept praying on what God was whispering on my heart and soul and in those moments of sweaty palms once again, being called, I had to share with our Chloe immediately! I will never forget it because it was this exact night where our dreams we never knew we had in us, came to life and became a part of our lifetime calling! God's calling! God helped me tell our daughter that night that we were going to start a boys and girls group that will meet once a month and bless our world. I asked her to name the group. She boldly and quickly spoke as if she was born knowing! Chloe quickly and calmly said "Star Girls", with a big smile stretched across her beautiful cheeks. I quickly and loudly said, "God's Star Girls!" I knew I had to throw in God! "Hello, this is God's Plan here"…we must include him!! We did go back and forth for a bit on the name, but praise God we both won! It was a dream come true!

Next our oldest son Breck named the boys group "God's Super Heroes". He too spoke the name reassuringly as if it was embedded on his body from birth! We started with gathering our children's friends, grandparents, and families. Together, hand in hand, we have been gifting our community monthly with simple blessings! We encouraged all girls to wear stars to remind them they are all God's Special Shining Stars! How great it was to see them shine as their hearts ideas and desires to bless others blew my ideas out of the park! Our boys loved spreading their blessings in their super hero capes, raking leaves for our grand elders, delivering plastic eggs filled with stickers for Acute Care Kids, and baking the best cake pops for our firemen. This group was a pure gift for all who gathered! Our children grew, and as homework piled up and activities pulled all families in a million directions, we were able to stop together in God's Lead and bless others in desperate need. Who would have thought there were so many children angels out there and parents and grandparents and friends and neighbors who are yearning to bless others on a daily basis, willing and ready but just need the opportunity! Just like the writing journey God had been taking me on, everything was lining into place in His Plan! This group has been one of the greatest gifts our family, friends and receivers have ever received! It's given us all a gift and opportunity to bless, encourage, lead, and change this world with goodness and light all for His Glory and for His children! We have been given the pleasure of serving God's people in magnificent ways by delivering handmade bible verse bookmarks, creating beaded bracelets for cancer patients, to helping others at the exact time they need it. This has been a calling which my heart is forever grateful for! If I hadn't risen from my hands and knees in prayer, our group may not have existed as it has since now grown larger, being re-named by Breck, "God's Messengers". This group is my gift and passion and is my heart's desire for everyone to start their own group and bless their community!

Just like writing, "God's Messenger's" became my Homework from above, and grew like His seeds that were planted in my heart, there was yet another delivery from God that blew in! It was the delivery of God's Hearts in such a beautiful way straight from heaven! God literally picked up my hands from my coat pockets and my purse, with camera in hand, and brought me to a complete STOP in my tracks to snap a photo of His Love, in the delivery of a heart! Yes, an actual heart. Spectacular hearts made just from our Heavenly Father! The first glimpse of His first heart, I will never forget and can remember on that Sunday afternoon my family and dear friends, the Buchfink's who surrounded me! This delivery dropped straight down from heaven and touched my eyes, heart and soul when it first caught my glance! It was a carved out red heart on the curbside of Subway! I stopped dead center in middle of the parking lot! God took my hands, leading them to snap a photo of this heart! His hearts came flooding down from heaven with such visibility and pure heavenly love! With each "sight seeing", they paused my every movement delivering His Beautiful love straight to my heart! These hearts began to speak out God's Love, His Forgiveness, His Grace, His Mercy, His Mighty Majestic Love for me!! With each one of His deliveries, every ounce of my soul couldn't wait to share with my family, closest angels, and friends!! My heart literally cried out in utter amazement and astonishment and thanksgiving to our Heavenly Father, as I can remember saying "Okay another one God! Wow! Thank you God!" It's as if with each heart discovery I immediately knew I needed to fold my hands in prayer and thanksgiving.

In the beginning, I would smile up at heaven when I would hear, "Mommy you stopped in traffic to take a picture of that tar heart. Mommy why are you taking a picture of that piece of pepperoni heart in my pizza? Heather, you are taking a picture of a leaf on the ground and almost made someone trip behind you" On more than one occasion, as crazy as it must have looked to an observer, these hearts touched our hearts in such a powerful way that only God can deliver! I remember one in particular that was spotted on one of my busiest "soccer Mom" days. I was running from one soccer field to the next, trying not to be late for next game. With our youngest in tow, I dropped the water jug and soccer ball immediately when I noticed a heart rock engraved by grass!! GOD had an amazing, glorious, majestic, powerful way of stopping every ounce of my body to see HIS LOVE in hearts, in all shapes and sizes, colors and textures! These were not normal hearts, these were His carved out hearts intended for all of His children to spot and to be filled up from head to toe with His Love for them! God has shown me oil spill hearts in a parking lot, our son Keegan's heart cookie that formed unexpectedly from his little bites as he saved for me from his preschool party, hearts from His shining rays of

Light bursting through our living room window, revealing the most beautiful heart projected on our ceiling, heart shaped fur spots on the back of a dog, and even a random heart leaf dangling from a tree blowing in the wind waiting, just waiting for all to notice and feel God's immediate love run through every vein in their body! God has a powerful way of stopping all of us in our tracks, stillness, grief, quietness, our solitude and joy and drawing our attention to HIS IMMEDIATE LOVE for us, and to receive His delivery in a heart has been more than breathtaking to say the least!

Sharing with others became an immediate action in my day! Not only did I begin sharing these hearts with such eagerness with my closest angels, family and friends, I began receiving many hearts from my loved ones in their surprise in return! These were Hearts that fell out of God's Palms for us all! How grateful we all are to receive God's Love in such a magical, beautiful way!! I am forever grateful to have received God's Grace that blew in like tumbleweeds after I became open for Him.

We've all heard that your dreams will come true with strong faith and a heck of a lot of hard work. Instead my friends, I leave you with this delivery from the bottom of my heart, "Once you kneel and surrender 100% of your entire being to our Heavenly Father, He will guide your every move as He molds you into your calling. He will be there in those dark times when you don't want to wear the shoes He lovingly chooses for you, but you will find yourself thanking Him in your dance together with the shoes He carefully chose just for you. He will continually and steadfastly bless you with the biggest gifts from heaven as you continue to surrender to Him on a dai-

At Book Bound By The Sea – 2016 Captiva Island, FL. My "Ready to Launch" moment, minutes after my feet hit the sand at Michelle's incredible workshop! Thank you, Michelle, for being the "Launch Pad" all of us authors have dreamed about!

ly basis. While you dance this journey hand in hand with our Heavenly Father, remember you can do all things in Christ who strengthens you! Your story is His, and He made yours a best seller!"

With His Love and Mine,
Heather Anderson ▓

HEATHER ANDERSON *was born in 1976 in Springfield Ohio. She currently resides in McKinney, TX with her amazing husband, their 3 beautiful children, and "Hope the Magnificent", their King Charles Cavalier.*

Heather enjoys family game nights and family road trips! She has a deep passion for jazz, a love for Christian music, Starbucks, and HGTV! Heather was formerly a teacher, nanny and Assistant Director at Primrose School of Wellington. She currently teaches at First Christian Church McKinney, and manages air show events with ADC Group. She created Faith & Hope Kreations, Christian art.

Heather is founder of "God's Messenger's", a group inspiring, encouraging, and leading children, friends and families together to bless our world. She is a positive, optimistic person always trying to look on "God's side of things". Her love of people and passionate faith became the foundation for her calling of Christian writing and her serving heart for all. Heather's heart's desire is to fill others with God's Faith and to inspire all to "Be Open" to God each day!

Heather Anderson
heather@withhisloveandmine.com
www.withhisloveandmine.org

2

Interrupted by Destiny;
Stepping into Faith
Sandra Antor

So what's wrong with me? I never dreamt that it would be this way. I never entertained the thought that I would be a spinster. An old lady with her cats, (I hate cats. Incidentally, I'm a dog person), no wonder it never occurred to me. I was busy living my life. College, Grad school, working, dating, traveling, a stint in the military and it never happened. According to all the movies and books I have seen or read, if you go about your regular day-to-day life you will meet "the one." You will meet "the one" in a classroom, grocery store, at the mall, car wash, laundry, airport, on a plane, at church, at a party, it just happens that way. But it didn't happen for me. After all of my travels and tossing to and fro, I looked up one day, and I was forty, single, never married with any children, not even a cat. So I had to wonder and ask myself, as one bold uncouth date asked me a few years prior, "So what's wrong with you?"

Really what's wrong with me? I am reasonably good looking, I'm no Halle Berry, but I'm not close to a dog either. I'm not a size six, but I'm not a size 16 either. And besides, I know dogs and heifers that have met "the one" and are happily married with children. So that physical stuff really does not matter to "the one". So I have this ongoing dialogue with myself while I am living my mundane life. And meanwhile, my family is asking the same question out loud. What's wrong? When are you going to have some babies? I knew it was getting bad because my family is super conservative Christians and they are not even asking, "When are you going to get married?" anymore. They're just asking me to have some babies. My sister and my mom were hearing my biological clock from the time I was 30. I did not tune into it until I turned forty. By that time, it sounded like Marisa Tomei in *My Cousin Vinny* stomping on the porch.

I regrouped and got focused. I made an appointment with my gynecologist who suggested that I may benefit from a consult with a fertility specialist. After a series of tests, I was told I had uterine fibroids that needed to be removed for me to have a chance to conceive and my fallopian tubes were occluded. The good news was that I had tons of healthy eggs for my age, which was surprising to the specialist. I was not surprised because my mother gave birth to my youngest brother at age 45. And he is mostly normal. Like my mother, I wanted to have a natural pregnancy. No petri dish, no injections, no pills. Just sex! I believed that once I had the fibroids removed, problem solved. Several months later I had them removed. Only I had no one to conceive with at that time. My gynecologist/surgeon recommended a hysterectomy because the fibroids were so numerous and my periods were so heavy they were making me anemic. I declined. I wanted children, my biological children. I wanted the whole pregnancy and sympathetic pregnancy experience. I wanted the baby shopping and baby shower experience. The water breaking and the 24 hours labor story experience. I wanted the motherhood experience. Isn't that what womanhood and being female is all about? I had a plan. I was going to find a man, get married, get pregnant and have a baby. I was going to do in the next 18 months what I was not able to do in the last 25 years.

One year later I was married. I go back to the fertility specialist with my husband so we both can be checked out. I redo the series of tests again; and received good news. My fallopian tubes are not occluded anymore. It was the fibroids that were pressing down on them and now that they have been removed I am 100% fertile. Only now I am 42 and due to my age getting pregnant may be difficult. Again the specialist is telling me all of this, and I am dismissing it because I know that women tend to inherit the fertility patterns of their mother. If your mother menopaused at 35, you would be likely to menopause at 35; if she was fertile until she was 50, you would likely be fertile until 50. I knew my mother was able to conceive at 45, so the physician's precautionary remarks did not apply to me. Enter my husband, seven years younger than me, and the epitome of good health; 6'2", and 175 pounds of pure muscle, looks like a model chiseled and ripped. His report comes back, and he has a low sperm count. The bastard is shooting blanks; I could not believe it. Ladies, never judge a book by its cover. Now I am so sure that God is playing me, and it's not funny. I had a picture in my mind of God saying, "Gotcha, you think you're going to make plans without consulting me!"

Meanwhile, I get a call from my sister Wendy. She's so excited on the other end of the phone I know something is up. She starts, "Girl I got a call from the State, they took Moses' baby (our cousin) and asked me to keep her. I have an idea."

At this, I began shaking my head thinking; there goes Lucy again. I know that whenever Wendy gets an idea involving me, she turns into Lucy (Lucille Ball), and I'm Ethel; meaning I am going to have a headache. I'm in trouble. Lucy has an idea, and it is going to be my problem later. I will have a dilemma from her "great idea".

She continued, "I'm going to keep the baby, and if you don't have a baby in a year, you can adopt her. It'll be perfect, and I'll make sure she's potty trained and ready for you."

At the time, the baby was approximately 18 months old. I was not paying any attention to my sister because, of course, I'll be pregnant in a year. My husband and I were newlyweds and we were actively trying to have a baby. My husband was on his medication, and I was doing my ovulation tests, and we were working my plan. I was not concerned because there was no reason why I would not be pregnant in a year.

A few weeks later my sister calls me and says, "Okay it's been a year, I'm ready to send the baby!"

Now I'm taken aback. Has it been a year? It seemed like only a few weeks ago. It's been a year. Panic start to set in. Oh My God, I'm not pregnant yet? What's wrong with me? Maybe the doctor was right? Am I too old to conceive naturally? I am dazed and in disbelief, so halfheartedly I conceded to taking the baby and started the adoption process.

In the interim, Lucy has another great idea. "We're going on a family cruise for a week, why don't you keep the baby. It'll be a good trial for you." Of all the ideas Lucy's had, this is not such a bad idea. If I am considering taking on the child full time, I should test my parenting skills and our compatibility first. So she drops the now two-and-a-half-year-old toddler off. The girl is wild, she's jumping on furniture, she has food everywhere, she does not respect boundaries, she touches everything, she doesn't listen, and she wears pull ups. This is not a good idea. I am 42 and lived alone until recently. I am not good with living things. I have no pets and no plants. I killed a fern when I was in college and had my first apartment. Do you know how hard it is to kill a fern? It is extremely difficult to kill a fern. In fact, I put the fern on life support a few times, and it came back. You can water it once a week, and it thrives. I managed to kill a fern. I have a black thumb. I killed a goldfish, the only pet I have had as an adult. The poor fish did not last one week with me. My two-year-old nephew was there at the time to witness Goldie's demise. I can still hear him asking in his baby voice; "Auntie Sandra, why you kill the fish? Why you kill the fish?"

At this point, I am rethinking this whole adoption thing. To make matters worse, unlike the fern or the goldfish, the child talks back. She can express her anger, her frustration, her needs,—NO, everything except that she wants to use the bathroom. She is unapologetically filling up that pull up regularly. I was starting to think she was doing it on purpose. Then I caught her—yes, red handed—I caught her squatting in the corner watching television ready to drop another load in her pull ups. I believe I startled her, "Get up and go to the potty." I felt vindicated; I knew she knew what she was doing.

My week trial was up, thank you, Jesus. We both survived, and I am so relieved. My sister picks her up and takes her home. Then something strange happens. I miss her. My husband and I proceed with adoption procedures. The State of Florida did a background check on both of us, fingerprints, home study, interview; we jumped through all the required hoops, and I passed. But there was a snag, something in my husband's background concerned the State, so they offered me the option to do a single parent adoption. I jumped on it. Little did the caseworker know that the single parent option was a blessing. Our marriage was beginning to be rocky already, and I had concerns about adopting a child with my spouse. So that snag was divine intervention.

Then we started playing the waiting game. The courts needed to assign custody to me so that the State of Florida can transfer the baby to my care. One month, we're still waiting; two months, we're still waiting; three months, we're still waiting; four months, we're still waiting. Then Lucy gets an idea, "I know what I'm going to do, the State is too comfortable, they're dragging their feet because they know the baby is in good hands. I'm going to call them and tell them I can't keep her anymore, so they need to have a hearing right away to place the child." It worked! A few weeks later I had custody of Destiny.

Now I never cared for the name Destiny; in my mind, it sounded like a girl that works the pole. Yes, like a "titty" bar stage name, an exotic dancer. So I selected a more appropriate name for my baby girl, Ariel. I thought that it was beautiful and not too common. By this time Destiny is between 30-38 months old. I would address her as Ariel when I'm giving her a bath, or feeding her or instructing her. She was not having it. She would ball her little fist and scream at the top of her lungs, "My name is DESTINY!!!" And so it is.

Adopting Destiny was the single most life-changing interruption to my life. Bigger than my marriage, bigger than joining the service, bigger than moving across the country. And the most wonderful thing that I have ever done. She has added a new dimension and perspective to my life. Being a parent is so intimate. Adoption was not my first choice or my second choice. It was not on my radar. I would encourage anyone who wants to have a family—and the traditional route is not happening for you—to adopt. Adoption is equally as rewarding. Do not deprive yourself or that child the love that you hold inside. From the day she came into my life, my life has never been the same; in the most awesome mind blowing way. Destiny's interruption into my life had been so transformative that when I got the call regarding the birth of her biological sister, there was no hesitation in my spirit. I eagerly stepped into faith and brought the newborn home at seven days old. And so she is named Faith.

Today I am the proud single parent of two beautiful adopted daughters. I could not imagine loving them anymore if they were my biological daughters. I recently reflected and concluded that if I lived another hundred years, I would probably not do anything more impactful than rearing these two little souls. Though my life was interrupted by Destiny, she taught me and prepared me to step into Faith. To God, Lucy, Destiny, and Faith I am ever grateful for the opportunity to serve as a mother.

SANDRA ANTOR. *The name Sandra is a variant of Alexander (the Great) meaning defender of mankind. I cannot help but to be my brother's keeper; for my name's sake. I am Sandra, defender of mankind. In my mind, I strive for self-actualization as Maslow terms it. This is who I am, virtuous and valuable; an original masterpiece, hand woven by The Creator Himself. Fearfully and wonderfully made, a dwelling place of the holy spirit of God. A true professional and leader. I am a registered nurse (RN) with a Bachelor's of Science degree in nursing. I hold a dual Masters, a MSN in nursing and an MBA degree with emphasis in healthcare management. Having served in the Surgeon General's Corps, I am an honorably discharged Lieutenant Commander. I value integrity, excellence and professionalism and aim to assist individuals and families in manifesting a more abundant quality of life. Mostly, above all my professional, academic and social accomplishments like my heroine, "I am my kids' mom".*

Sandra Antor
sandraantor@yahoo.com
305-785-5856

3

Journey to Joy
Ruth Megli Boettger

Can I tell you a story? It's all about relationships. It's about travel, my journey, and joy.

> "What day is it?" asked Pooh.
> "It's today," squeaked Piglet.
> "My favorite day," said Pooh.

Loving my tramp (a New Zealand hike) out amidst the pine trees, hills, streams and birds, I smile like a silly baboon. In this beautiful country on the south island of New Zealand, I have found a precious paradise right here where I've landed. I sing out loud, feeling a joyous release, a familiar tune that is going through my head "I'm a child of the king who made everything".

Views like this still take my breath away. Walking on soft pine needles one moment and a hard path the next, the unknowns that are just around the next bend keep me walking...up the hill, down the next and across a stream. Suddenly, I stop. It hits me. This is so much like my journey of life!

Not totally aware of what brought me here to this land of beauty, I pause right here on the hill to catch my breath and reflect as I enjoy the amazing views of the green expanse of native trees and a city in the far distance. Maybe it's the search...the empty spaces in my life where it was once so full…my neediness…my lack of direction…my loss of dreams…

Somehow, I feel a strong tug to search and discover new avenues to explore my questions. I need to pursue and reach beyond the usual so that I can again adventure and live!

Never dreaming what was around the next bend, my life was interrupted by the death of my soul mate, Delbert, my one true love.

It took us so long to find each other, and we thoroughly enjoyed life together. However, suddenly in one day it was gone. Well, not gone because life will forever be richer but it has radically changed. Leaving a humongous gaping hole, for our son, Rueben and I, it became important to find some answers as I searched for purpose, a new plan and a path to follow.

"IF there comes a day when we can't be together, keep me in your heart…I'll stay there forever." Winnie the Pooh

Reading was one way for me to work through my huge loss and to stay healthy and happy. So, I read tons of books. I read all kinds of books. A book called "One Yes At a Time" made sense to me, since I couldn't seem to see ahead to plan the big picture. Rueben and I had decided that since life had drastically changed for both of us, it would have to look a lot different and so we determined to embrace change.

A quote I had on our bulletin board for months was by Dr. Seuss — *'Don't cry because it's over, smile because it happened.'*

"He is a wise man who does not grieve for the things which he has not, but rejoices for those which he has." Epictotus

A major decision to home school (an "off the wall" venture, in our minds) for Rueben's Grade 11 and 12 included travel as part of his education. So we did trips together with my mom, with friends and also spent time with his cousins. I was already beginning to see how we were saying "yes" to move out of our comfort zone. We were saying "yes" to change.

After graduating, Rueben planned a trip of a lifetime "Down Under" to be a part of the harvest crew for my brother in Australia and then do the Outdoor Adventure plus Bible Course at a Capernwray School in New Zealand. So then came my big"YES"to joining him on this trip.

"Yes"to spending time with my son, AND my Australian family,
"yes"to reconnecting with my parents' friends in N.Z.,
"yes"to stepping way out of my comfort zone,
"yes"to living in faith and not fear,
"yes"to making new friends, to the unknown and to adventure!

Invited to come stay at my brother's property in Australia for three months, Rueben would experience brand new jobs, people and places. I would, well, umm, perhaps find some volunteer work, maybe explore, and try to make some connections.

Hoping I hadn't left too many blanks in the schedule, we left, eager to embark on new territory (but personally battling the feeling of leaving loose ends with financial, physical and emotional needs). Arriving in Australia to a warm welcome from my brother and his wife, we settled in happily and became part of the hub of activity at the"Kelso"property. Dale and Leslie run a busy operation with cropping, cattle and horses on the place. We experienced teamwork happening in a fun and caring culture. They work hard but it wasn't just about the work…relationships were healthy and strong.

"A single act of kindness throws out roots in all directions and the roots spring up and make new trees."
Amelia Earhart

With community choir, a ladies study, Sunday Church and a soup kitchen for the aboriginals each week, I experienced community life. Conversations on the 40-minute drives to town, at morning coffees with the whole station, and"tea"every night with Dale and Leslie were priceless times of sharing thoughts and sorting out ideas for me.

Driving back from the soup kitchen at sunset was surreal. Adding to the glorious sunset colors were dozens and dozens of kangaroos hopping over and beside the road at every bend giving me plenty of reason to take my time, feel in touch with a bigger picture and enjoy nature's entertainment.

Vacation to the glorious beaches of Australia with Rueben was an amazing time of bonding and fun. The ocean, sand, sun and the huge bonus of my son being there was healthy for my body, soul and mind. Christmas with my niece, Kim, her husband, Simon, and their wee Ellie, also all made for beautiful memories. I felt connected, loved, accepted, and in a good place to grow strong. I see again that relationships take effort, planning, and time…just like everything else in life that is worthwhile, precious and meaningful.

We departed knowing that this was a once in a lifetime experience for both of us. Spending quality time with family is never wasted. The bond has been built stronger. Spending a few days in Sydney, we reflected back on how the time flew. We never once felt it was too long.

"No moment is useless, no day void when shaped by the creative power of love." Sally Clarkson.

Continuing to reflect, I dangle my feet in a cool stream just down from the path. Australia was about seeing My Creator God providing for my physical, emotional and spiritual needs.

Three months later, landing in Auckland, N.Z. Rueben and I were privileged to spend more quality time together. Hunting cars is not my thing, but it is his so I can enjoy it through his eyes. Neither is sleeping in a tent but meeting all those interesting travelers from Germany and France in the campgrounds sharing tips and experiences they've had is fun. And so we ate simple, and felt healthy in the great outdoors using Rueben's adequate camping equipment. One morning looking for food, we suddenly found ourselves in a totally different culture, surrounded by Maori people in an outdoor market. Just the two of us, doing things we would not be doing at home together.

> "A good relationship has a pattern like a dance which
> is endlessly changing in its unfolding."
>
> **Anne Morrow Lindbergh**

Driving out to Raglan, the best surfing beach in N.Z., to reconnect with my parent's good friends, Ralph and Judith, we were warmly taken in. Rueben pitched his tent in the garden and I got the guest room across from Molly, Ralph's daughter from England, who happened to be visiting the same week. We spent hours catching up on the drama of our lives since the teen years.

A week later, back at Auckland we picked up two of Rueben's school friends, Lukas and Emily, who joined us for the last week before their school started. Previously, I had some huge hesitations but ended up thoroughly enjoying this week with three 18 year olds! It brought back memories of an era in life that is all about adventure, challenge, food, fun, and just a few fears. Spontaneity ruled the day. We found lots of adventure on our trip around the Colonial Peninsula digging hot tubs in the sand, swimming the Cathedral Cove, and cliff diving at Hoffman's pool close to Thames.

We had arranged to meet John and Cara through friends from home (Lukas' family). This strong community minded Kiwi couple invited us in for a barbeque the first night and then proceeded to plan an intense day of hiking up to the Pinnacles for a group of nine including Lukas' three very energetic young cousins. The hike was meant to be an overnighter but we did it in one day! Hiking seems to bring to light previously undisclosed character traits as one deals with the pressures of the tramp and the dynamics of the group. A strained foot muscle kept me recalling it for weeks. It was stunningly beautiful as well as intense.

The last day in this area, the boys went with John who checks traps every two weeks for the rodents who threaten the national Kiwi bird population in this region. We could never have seen or learned a fraction of what we did without a connection with this lovely couple.

Dropping off my young and fun companions at school, leaving me without play mates, brought a whole new series of emotions and set of decisions. Knowing that I could use someone to bounce off my ideas, I headed back to our friends at Raglan for a couple of days to get my emotional fix and feel safe and comfortable for another few days.

In total, I spent only three nights in guest houses or hotels. The hotel in Hamilton was noisy and busy and there are no faces, no conversations that stick in my memory. The guest house in Wellington literally had a scary face making me very uneasy for the whole evening and night. I returned from going out after dark, to get a freshly made Indian naan bread down the street and dragged the big chiffonier in front of the door. I'm sure there was no danger but somehow I felt vulnerable. Later on my travels, I found the guest house in Nelson was much more comfortable plus by then perhaps I felt more secure overall. The rest of my trip is full of connections and memories of forming friendships. The connections I made proved to make life meaningful, purposeful, interesting and at the same time very unpredictable!

Relationship building was part of my plan. As I hopped onto the bus en route to the ferry, which would take me to the South Island, I had a great opportunity to chat with a young Maori fellow on his way back to the military base. He had left his wife and two children home in Auckland. My understanding of their language, history and culture grew. Then sitting on the 3-hour ferry ride, I met a young Chinese gal from the Philippines who had worked at the Gold Coast in Australia for a year. It was fascinating to hear about her dreams and to see how brave she was. At the ferry terminal, I waited with a gal from Holland whose traveling partner had to return to her grandpa's funeral and on the next bus trip it was a gal from Spain working on a farm. Reaching a destination near Christchurch, where I had a connection through my past jewelry business, was very reassuring. It was a good place to start exploring the South Island.

Bev was full of surprises. She was the absolute best promoter of the South Island I could have found and the best tour guide ever. The first two weeks as Bev shared her farmhouse, time, hobbies and friends with me, I learned a lot about N.Z. and about relationships.

Bev lost her husband around the same time I had lost mine! She taught me card making, took me golfing and "coffeeing" with her friends. As I watched her connecting with relationships she had built up over the years I appreciated the strength and tenacity with which she tackled her daily life.

Touring the south part of the Island with Bev was a time for snapping pictures of awesome scenery and meeting her friends and family. Bev's friends close to Invercargil kept us for a couple of days, giving us time to explore with a home base. The minute we arrived at the old farmstead and met, I felt like I'd come upon royalty. I could have listened and watched "Queen Rosalund" all day long. I loved eating in their farm kitchen with the "King" and the "Prince" both adding to the jovial atmosphere. I could see their respect for each other and sense humor with which they all looked at life. They were the most down-to-earth, real, genuine people you could ever meet and yet in my head they have forever stayed royalty.

I would have never found the places we saw and met the people we stayed with on my own. I appreciated enormously this connection and friendship with Bev.

A WILD IDEA

At some stage, I realized that I was not ready to go back home. I was enjoying the adventure even as it tested my courage and stamina. I knew I could learn so much more. This was especially true when I found out about a website called "workaways". This would give me the opportunity to stay with New Zealanders and work for my keep while exploring the area where they lived. It would also challenge me to live by faith and not fear! I think this is what N.Z. was about for me…to trust in a caring competent God instead of living in fear of the unknown, of the big changes that kept coming, or of my inadequacies.

My first "workaway" was across the other side of the Island at Greymouth with "Tara and the gang". It was intimidating for me when I found I was to be with young girls. It was also their first workaway experience so I think we made up all our own rules and it worked fine. I felt like

I was living inside the covers of a book about a very entertaining Irish family. Nina Mia is a very capable, musical 10 year old with long red hair who is thinking she's already a teen, Pyper is a very relational lovable 9 year old who loves animals, Sorcha is an adorable 7 year old who loves gardens, caterpillars and eating good things like the cucumbers and blackberries growing out of the back door. Their parents, Jax and Tara, are laid back, hospitable, have a great sense of humor, like their alcohol, have strong accents and are delightfully Irish! I lived in a nice private sleep out at the back and dove in through the back door of the house when I needed a washroom. My job was to drive the girls to school, pick them up, and take them to their activities…with a Jaguar! While they were in school, I had the "Jag" to explore. And explore I did. My two favorite spots were south to Hokitika (fun beaches and lake country) and north to the Pancake Rocks (rough ocean, blow holes and forest walks). Weekends and evenings, I was free to be part of the family so I joined in watching movies on TV, took the girls to the beach and went to their motorbike rally at two beach side hotels with big decks onto the sand. It was a lovely place to spend the evening and meet their friends. I loved watching how Jax and Tara took time to be with the girls, telling them stories as they went to bed. I would go to the sleep out and listen to the ocean roar. It was very hard to pull myself away after two weeks.

One day while strolling on Mahera Quay in Graymouth, I met a young Chinese lady who seemed lost. She was looking for the open ocean so I took her with me to get my groceries then drove her out of town and parked close to a beach. Passing by a horse in the paddock, she asked if she could touch it having never been this close to one before. Topping a knoll, we stood at the ocean's edge, where she stood still, staring. I can still see the raw emotions and her amazement at the views stretching in at least three directions right to the horizon. She explained that in China, she would see only skyscrapers.

Heading to a sunnier spot, I took a bus to my next workaway place on the north part of the South Island where beautiful orchards fill the countryside. Here, I stayed with Jane who lost her partner eight years before after starting their bed and breakfast unit out of their home. It was very earthy, homey and creative there. I stayed out in the camper van, which was more private than the guest room. It made me feel close to the beautiful outdoors and I'd never stayed in one before! My job was to take care of the guest suite, do some gardening and cook supper for when Jane got home from work. There was a bike for my use so I peddled the 5 km into Motueka every day enjoying the orchards (and hills!) on the way.

One morning turned ugly and foul quickly when I spilled the wee pee bucket on myself. However, after cleaning up, I decided to carry on with the day which entirely and completely turned into a gorgeous "joy memory" spent in the Park!

Never will I forget the three days of hiking in the Abel Tasman National Park. Catching the bus just outside the gate then taking a water taxi to a variety of different long walks, I explored absolutely gorgeous pathways, native lush forests, brilliant blue water and warm white sandy beaches. I don't even know how to describe the vibrant colors, the peacefulness, the joy of walking in the warm fresh air, the sounds of birds calling to each other in the stillness of the forest, sounds of lapping waves, and the fun of not knowing who you will meet on the trail. It was another surreal experience. Feeling a tad bit lonely on my second day in the Park, I came to a deserted beach. As I swam back from the sand island, a friendly Kiwi family appeared and invited me into their holiday house for coffee. It was an unexpected pleasure to be invited into their space and enjoy an afternoon with a delightful family.

While in this area, I celebrated Delbert's birthday and our anniversary date. Poignant memories were strong, while I sat on a patio sipping a latte at the corner café. I realized deeply the meaningfulness of good relationship and appreciated anew all my connections from past years as well as the new ones that I was forming. Somehow soaking in the beauty of nature all around me, brings me closer to eternity, more aware of how deep relationships go and how this is what life is really all about.

Loving this area but not having another spot lined up, I was stressing a bit until one evening, Jane picked up the phone, called a friend she worked with and found he was looking for someone to come stay. Assuring me that he was a very nice gentleman, she left to see her parents in Fiji. Alex picked me up in his beat up farm truck, tossing my suitcase and I into the back seat. My nose wrinkling to the smell of dog in front and garbage behind, we headed to the dump and then to the fish wharf to buy fresh fish for dinner that night. It turned out that he was a chef! I couldn't dream up a better time than being served a gourmet meal each night, taking Eva (the golden retriever) on walks and gardening on a beautiful piece of land along the river.

At times, it was tempting to stay with this gentle man who seemed to find me attractive even in my garden attire and enjoyed my company. But I cannot step out of my real world and make this more than temporary, I must move on.

So here I am sitting on a hill enjoying the perspective from a distance.

I was thinking how I miss Delbert more than ever when I travel. However, it is priceless to be able to step into people's lives and see from a different perspective. I feel incredibly blessed that so many have opened their spaces and their hearts to me.

So I did move on. A phone call to introduce myself to friends of the "Royal Family" (a contact they gave me when we stayed with them on the south island tour) brought an invite to come stay! I felt an immediate connection. They warmly took me into their home, took me everywhere I needed to go and introduced me to their friends (Rodney, an English entrepreneur and Norma, a lovely Scot). Rodney had an outdoor oven and a tub heated with solar power I'm still wishing I could experience.

I found out John has a kidney transplant done 20 years ago that was to only last 7 years and Margaret had half a lung left. And yet they enjoy life and focus on what they do have, which are friends and family, a good marriage relationship and a lovely place in the country with gardens. I left feeling that a strong bond of friendship was built and I miss my coffee outings with them dreadfully.

This was Easter time and I was feeling like family time would be nice. So when I heard from my niece, Katy Sue and her friend, Anna, that they were heading my way, I jumped at the opportunity to connect for a few days and share my favorite spots. We spent our nights in a hostel, and our days biking and tramping. We also did a traveling supper one night of Thai, Indian and Malaysian food. Very fun and full!

Leaving by bus to Picton, where the ferry would take me to the North Island, the only empty seat was filled with stuff but I plunked myself down, feeling quite unwelcome. Very soon Rutha from Wyoming, U.S.A. seemed like a friend. An older very fit lady, I found her lifestyle very fascinating. She comes to NZ every year participating in the WWOOF program (world wide opportunities on organic farms) and goes back "home" to a camping lifestyle. I'm smiling and nodding at her stories. Right now, I can relate to her enjoying life that way and I realized that I quite enjoy living a more simple, uncluttered life.

I chose Waheiki Island for my last workaway because I had mental images of a luxury week and some posh living as I planned the bus trips and ferry rides out to the small island. It didn't turn out easy but ended up better than easy. It was real life. Hard. I lived in a rudimentary cabin, had a rat visitor one night, an outdoor toilet and shower and thought that I wouldn't stay long. I'm so glad I decided to stay because I experienced amazing tenacity, determination, and energy from Katherine, who is working towards a gigantic dream. Pulling heritage buildings onto the property to use for accommodation, they had started with vineyards, a wine cellar/barn and a big lodge. I will never forget my time there. The highlights for me were sitting at my table in the cabin with Katherine, a salad, a bottle of wine and a conversation that lasted all evening... getting ready for guests at the big lodge when a gentleman from Mongolia arrives ahead of time to chat...organizing the barn which was a "Hoarder's Den"...working as a team with Alex O'Le, from Germany, a "workawayer" like me (but young!), and forging a wonderful friendship in which we shared meals plus great conversations morning and evening, and our day off exploring the beaches...going to a wedding with Katherine and letting her doves fly away back home...facing some of my fears...ending up loving an outdoor shower...realizing that because I am loved, I can love, and I always have something to give. Heading back to Auckland on the ferry, I waved goodbye with mixed emotions, but joy came through strong.

Finishing my N.Z. time with Ralph and Judith at Raglan, I could relax and walk the beaches, visit and catch up on the last adventurous months. In a few days I was back on the bus heading to Hamilton to stay with Nathan and Maida, in a deluxe suite with lovely gardens everywhere, lunches, coffees and talks, and finally a ride to Rueben's school. I got my luxurious living after all that last week as well as special time spent with two sets of my parents' good friends!

Rueben took an afternoon off to drive me back to Auckland. Left at the airport, I suddenly felt huge pangs of loneliness. I was leaving so much behind with so many memories of beautiful people and unique experiences over the past months. But I know that there are precious family and friends on the next part of the journey also. So home I fly to safe, strong ties that hold me while I keep growing, learning and solving my unique set of problems. I am so grateful for my friends and family that "do life" with me. I have a "board of directors" (some of which are not even aware that they are on my board!) that help me handle life and are crucial to my successes. My bridges are built, and I must work at keeping them strong. A special friend reminded me lately that we must "mend fences and not hold on to hard feelings".

> **"Reflect upon your present blessings, of which every man has plenty; not on your past misfortunes, of which all men have some."**
>
> **Charles Dickens**

ANOTHER WILD IDEA

Somewhere along the way, or after I returned home, an idea to join airbnb.ca was born. It took off full flight and we're flying!

> **"Home is more about cultivating a heart for people, than having a physical dwelling."**

I am hosting people at my home through a website called airbnb. ca, to accommodate families and friends for their get-to-gathers and rendezvous. It is delightful and inspiring to have groups here that are being creative (quilting retreats), traveling through, groups forming a lasting family bond (marriages and reunions), and groups spending time rebooting (young moms get-away and mom with daughters to do shopping). So perhaps on your travels, you'd like to join me here close to Calgary, Alberta, Canada (an hour from the Rocky Mountains) on a quiet country, sunny, spacious acreage home! Email me at bertruth@gmail. com or check out airbnb.ca.

So I continue my journey, hiking up and down hills, stopping at times to enjoy the views on the way. At times, I take a side trip to explore the path of the sparkly tumbling stream and the way feels sunny and happy, at other times cloudy and sad with regrets. I keep on walking and around the bend joy shows up! Perhaps we will meet on YOUR journey to joy! ▓

RUTH MEGLI BOETTGER.

Growing up in a solid family and a close-knit community, Ruth has always had a passion and propensity to build strong relationships. Being single for many years gave her opportunities to travel, sing, work in small business and in the Corporate World. A joyful surprise in life was meeting Delbert and creating her own loving, fun family building on her strong family values. Losing her husband has given her another dimension of recognizing that everyone needs to be in good relationships.

Ruth is mom to a precious boy (now a young man)! She values being a friend, a daughter, a sister and an auntie. She is aware of being a child of God, and a traveler on a journey to joy. Knowing she is deeply loved, she can love others and give from her heart, dream big dreams and write her stories.

She takes people into her acreage home near Calgary, Alberta, Canada (close to the Canadian Rockies) through airbnb.ca to share her space and her heart, connecting with people from all over the world. Her philosophy is that meeting people and building relationships is a key to enjoying life.

Ruth Megli Boettger
bertruth@gmail.com
403-512-2788

4

Seeing Through the Window
Judith Canterbury

I had worked in adult day services for over 20 years. I was and still am considered a leader in this field. I was the executive director of a non-profit organization operating two adult day programs for the care of persons with Alzheimer's disease and related disorders. I started this particular organization 13 year earlier with the help of a group of psychiatrists.

We originally opened a day program that was predominately operated by volunteers. Over the 13 years that the organization was in business, our board grew as well as the services we provided. Our budget was over a million dollars a year with $300,000 to $400,000 a year raised through grants that I wrote.

The board did well at determining how to utilize funds from a large bequest. The board members decided that we needed to find a better location for one of the centers and helped find just the right building. I found low interest funding available to nonprofits to supplement the purchase and renovation costs and the board found individuals in the community to support the renovation of the building. I felt like the board and staff were on the same mission.

Issues on the board began to arise when some board members retired and new members came on. The new individuals had ideas and desires that were not in line with the original board's vision. Conflicting visions split the board's purpose.

As the conflicts increased, staff, including me, began to feel the strain. The new board members would demand information in ways that staff had not provided in the past. They would then complain that they did not understand the information we were providing. Since the new members were not business people, they had a great deal of difficulty understanding the financial information and reports that we had always used.

It was difficult trying to manage the constant barrage of questions from these new board members as well as the day-to-day business of the program. Deadlines for reports to the State and other oversight agencies were compromised. We were at a stage in the growth of the agency where staff was stretched thin and more staff was needed, but the new board members were opposed to adding any new positions. For the staff, the safety of our clients was utmost in our minds.

My stress was increasing daily, and I began to have more evidence of that through physical manifestations such as, headaches, heart flutters and poor sleep. I knew mentally and physically, that I was not going to be able to continue with the level of harassment the new board members were placing on the staff.

During this period, several of my long-term board members became frustrated with the conflicts. As volunteers, they felt that they could not continue to work in an environment where every decision had to be discussed and argued. The old board members felt that many of the questions being asked involved decisions that should be made by staff and not the board. As a result, long-term members on the board began resigning, not wanting to deal with this type of conflict. It left a majority of those who were causing the disruption.

Feeling abandoned and overwhelmed, I contacted an attorney in the area who provided dispute resolution services to boards and staff of non-profits. After a discussion with him, I approached the board and requested we meet with him to try to resolve the issues that were continually disrupting the daily operations of the program. Their answer was an emphatic "No," even when I offered to donate the funds to pay for the workshop.

I knew that I could not continue to work in such a hostile environment. I had always been a very positive individual, knowing that whatever I wanted to do I could accomplish. I was extremely frustrated. I was sad and angry. This was my life's work and I felt as if the individuals on the board had no idea of the original goal of the program or mission of the program. Their whole purpose seemed to be finding fault and making new work for staff.

Finally, I realized that because of my health, there was no way that this was going to work out. I called the attorney that had offered to work with the staff and board to come to some resolution. I asked him to help me sever my relationship from the organization, in an as amenable way as possible.

The attorney reminded me that sometimes things happen that we see as "bad," but there may be something better around the corner. He reminded me of the old adage, "When God closes a door he always opens a window." I agreed that I could not stay, and he was able to help me negotiate my exit from the organization in such a way that I felt they were left in the best position possible.

Okay, so now what do I do? Sure, I have been out of work before. I had even left positions where I felt that I had been a crucial part of the organization. However, in some ways, I felt emotionally elated because I knew I no longer had to deal with the conflicts. Nevertheless, I was also emotionally drained from the past several months of dealing with those conflicts.

One day when I was feeling particularly down, and trying to decide what to do next, I picked up the phone and called a very good friend. She gave me some of the best advice ever. She told me to look at all of my experience. She said I have more experience in this field than anyone she knew. What about trying consulting work? I had consulted for free with many programs over the years, sharing my knowledge to help others start programs. Maybe I should try charging for my "expertise."

As it turned out, the field of adult day services was in the beginning stages of an explosive growth. The problem was there were not very many consultants available to help individuals who were interested in starting programs. I soon found out that some of those "consultants" had no idea of what they were doing.

As I mentioned, I had done consulting in the past, with individuals who were interested in trying to start a program similar to the one we ran. We would invite them to come and see our program. We discussed ideas on how to develop their policies and procedures, shared forms as samples for their programs, provided information on funding sources and generally shared our knowledge of what we were doing.

How can I do the consulting thing and make money? I was well connected with the State staff who oversaw the start-up of programs as well as many other people in the field. I thought maybe I should put out the word that I was interested in helping individuals start a center. I might get a few calls. So I started figuring out how much to charge. What could I charge people for? I thought about what I knew and how to put together a package that would help others. I picked a name for my business, Canterbury Consulting, printed some business cards, developed a price list of services, wrote up a simple one-page contract, and was ready to go.

I began to get calls immediately. The minute I had mentioned to my friend that consulting did sound like a good idea, she began to put out the word. The people who called were from all walks of life, some of whom had never been in health services before. I was always interested in why someone would want to start a business helping older adults and the disabled. I tried to screen out clients that were looking at this business strictly from a monetary point of view. I had been in health care long enough to know that when a service becomes popular and starts growing, there are always unscrupulous people around to take advantage. It had happened most recently with the durable medical equipment business, resulting in the waste of millions of fraudulent dollars. I did not want to be a contributing factor to fraud in the area I had worked in for so long.

Within three months, I had to hire a young lady who had once been my administrative assistant when I ran the nonprofit. She had changed jobs and wasn't happy where she was working. She loved the idea of doing something similar to what we had done before. One of the first meetings we attended was for potential providers in the Los Angeles area. At that meeting, we encountered two ladies who had hired a "consultant," paid her thousands of dollars, and had absolutely nothing to show for it two months later. We then realized that not everybody on either the consultant or owner side of starting a program were entirely honest or competent.

We took these ladies through the startup process. They had real "heart" for the population that they wanted to serve. As Russian immigrants themselves, they knew that many of the services available to frail, elderly clients did not have providers who spoke the language or understood the culture of the Russian elderly. As a result, this was the first population that they chose to serve. Their center serves not only the Russian elderly, but they discovered that other centers were not serving some segments of the population, including the younger disabled. They asked me to help train their staff on cultural issues and hire individuals who were knowledgeable about working with younger disabled or other cultures. Today, their center is prospering and providing much needed care services to a variety of individuals.

I soon realized that the loss of something I worked so hard to achieve was an opportunity. God had definitely opened a window. Had I stayed with the nonprofit, I would most likely have had irreparable health problems, been totally frustrated and possibly divorced since my husband was also frustrated with my inability to see what was happening to me as a result of the stress. When I decided to become a consultant, my husband pointed out the possibilities. He asked "How many families are impacted at the day care and how many families can be impacted through consulting with new start-ups?"

I took the attorney's advice and let go of things I could not control. When I trusted all would be right, and that constant frustration no longer blinded me, my vision of things cleared up and I soon realized why I was chosen to go through this ordeal. As a result of starting a consulting business, 150 additional centers were opened to serve individuals who wanted to stay in their own homes and avoid a nursing home, or die early due to a lack of care.

At the nonprofit, we were serving about 100 families a year. The 150 centers were serving about 15,000 families a year. Most of the clients being served were individuals who would have "fallen through the cracks", if an adult day health care program had not opened in their neighborhood.

This change was also a life saver for the young lady I hired. She was always a hard worker. When we worked at the nonprofit, she helped with everything from fundraising, grant writing and management to going out on the floor and helping someone who was confused and lost. To watch her grow and mature into a knowledgeable woman was very satisfying for me. About a year after she began working for me, she became pregnant and had her only child.

Being a mom in a wheelchair is hard enough, but she could not bear the thought of putting the baby in day care. Therefore, we structured our office, which was in my home, around him. He set our hours and went on site visits. As a result, today he has grown into a bright young man.

My assistant has now become my colleague. She has grown in knowledge and is now the administrator of two of the programs that we helped start. She is well respected in the field and a real asset to the agencies she works with.

So when you are faced with a situation that just seems beyond your strength to endure, step back. Look around and ask yourself if this stress is healthy or hurting you. If the answer is the latter, don't hold onto that job for the sake of security, prestige, or fear of failure. When you no longer have your eyes blinded by all the worry and frustration, you just may see through that window.

JUDY CANTERBURY MSN, GNP, RN

Canterbury Consulting, Inc. Judy Canterbury has worked more than 39 years in the field of adult day services, where she has been a program nurse, program director and administrator in Adult Day Programs, Alzheimer's Day Care Resource Centers and Adult Day Health Care Centers. She started four adult day centers herself and helped others through her consulting business. Today, she and her business partner operate a community outreach program with nursing services for young adults with moderate to severe intellectual and developmental disabilities. They have also started a nonprofit agency to provide supportive services to adults with intellectual and developmental disabilities living independently.

Judy holds a Master's of Science in Nursing, is a Geriatric Nurse Practitioner and a Registered Nurse. She a Member of the California Association for Adult Day Services. She served as a Region Director and Secretary of the National Adult Day Services Association. She is well respected in the field of adult day services and as an advocate, speaking at legislative hearings, knocking on lawmaker's doors and working in the community. Photography has become a passion and social media keeps her in touch with 7 grandchildren and 7 great grandchildren.

Judith "Judy" Canterbury
judycan41@gmail.com
7604195224

5

Hope Through Conversations
Rose Colarossi

Conversations can truly enhance and change someone's life and help to grow their business. Rose Colarossi has chosen to transform herself multiple times over the years to adjust to her family's needs... By building relationships, and having a strong work ethic, Rose has been very successful at growing her businesses. She now wants to use **conversations** and relationships to spread awareness about social issues in an effort to educate, prevent and foster participation and change. Rose also wants to use **conversations** to support, inspire and empower other Women Entrepreneurs.

What is your purpose? How do you find solutions? Do you believe **conversations** are important or a waste of time? I believe that purpose and solutions are often found through **conversation**. If you are like me, you have had multiple purposes throughout your life and have gone searching for many solutions.

While attending college, I worked in marketing departments of several large corporations. I obtained my first job after having a **conversation** with a friend's mother. I learned of each one of my jobs through **conversations**. Marketing and Promotion came very easy to me and I enjoyed it. However, I was torn between a business degree and a degree in Psychology. During a long **conversation** with a college professor that I respected, I learned about a work-study program in which I could be trained in behavior modification and work with children who had autism. I trusted his insight and I fell in love with the field, the children and families I worked with. I knew immediately that my purpose was to help children and their families unite and thrive.

When I married my husband, my purpose was not only as a wife, but to be a loving and supportive stepmother. After having our younger son and daughter, my purpose was to be the best mom I could be.

When I was pregnant with my youngest, my husband was offered an opportunity to relocate with his company to Dallas, Texas. Two weeks later, we welcomed our youngest daughter. It was a whirlwind. My husband's job required him to travel Monday through Friday. We had left all of our family in New York and I now had a newborn. Our newborn daughter suffered from a terrible case of reflux. She had to be kept upright all the time and would spike high fevers and catch viruses. She did not sleep for more than four hours at a time. Our three year old didn't know what was going on. We had moved him away from everyone he knew and not only did we introduce a new baby, we introduced one that cried all the time and needed constant attention. I knew in my gut that reflux could not be the only problem, but every doctor I took her to diagnosed her the same way. We were at the emergency room so often, that the nurses and most of the doctors knew us all by name.

Determined to find an answer, I would talk to any doctor or nurse that would listen. Through a **conversation** with one of the emergency room doctors, he told me about a pediatric gastroenterologist at Children's in Dallas by the name of Dr. Anderson. Immediately after meeting with us, Dr. Anderson ordered several tests on Kelly. The tests revealed that my daughter's body could not break down proteins and that she was not thriving. I felt helpless. I had tried breastfeeding and I had tried every type of hypoallergenic formula on the market. Nothing worked. Dr. Anderson told me about a trial involving the use of an intravenous formula from France, taken orally. He drove to Houston the next day to get samples and had me meet him at his house that weekend. *Yes. At his house and on a Sunday.* I went home and prepared the formula and it worked! It was a liquid miracle. I am forever grateful to him for going above and beyond to help us. Kelly slept for seven hours for the first time since she was born. No more crying baby. She was finally thriving! Life was as it should be.

About a year before Kelly was to start kindergarten, our oldest son was about to enter college and our oldest daughter was entering a boarding school. We needed another income, so I started looking for a job. However, my first priority was to be there for my children. After a **conversation** with the owner of a fitness franchise, several **conversations** with other owners and members, and much research, I decided to open my own club. The hours afforded me to be home before and after school and they were closed on Sunday. Little did I know that what I was about to embark on would be much more than just a fitness center. This was a business not only about weight loss, but about healthy choices, fears, self-esteem, life style changes, perception, relationships, etc. My team and I strived to provide an uplifting and safe environment for all of our members. Relationships were forged every day through **conversations** both on and off the circuit. We had members of all ages and backgrounds. The **conversations** over the years were incredibly educational, motivating and inspiring. We experienced one another's triumphs and losses. It was an incredible experience.

Our oldest son came to us with a proposal. He wanted us to invest in a restaurant concept in Dallas that he would manage. He had been managing a location in Colorado and was very successful. My husband and I had many **conversations** with one another, our son, the CEO and the CFO, and, of course, conducted our due diligence. We ultimately decided that it was a great brand and that it would be a good investment for our retirement. We were also thrilled that our son would be moving back to Dallas.

The Egg & I Restaurant in North Dallas/Addison opened in July 2008. Two months after the restaurant opened, our son and his wife gifted us with our first grandson. It was an exciting and happy time for all of us. Life was great. Then, in October, 2008 the stock market crashed. Our growing business stopped growing. Consumers were cutting back on anything considered an extra expense. In mid-December 2008, we tragically lost my brother. It was a devastating time to say the least. I stayed in New York for a few weeks after his funeral, caring for my mother and another family member.

Within an hour of returning home to Dallas, I received a call from our bank informing me that our restaurant had been the subject of Internet fraud. The bank would be opening an escrow account for all monies collected from our customers via credit cards until it was proven that we were not responsible. I was told that we would have to get a ten thousand dollar cashier's check and hire a forensic investigator to determine who was at fault. As you can imagine, my head was spinning. I called a family meeting with my husband, daughter-in-law and son and told them that we already had too many losses and that we were not going to have any more. They agreed. We knew that we would all have to make sacrifices but together we could get through this. Our son did not take a salary and he cut expenses anywhere he could at the restaurant. My husband and daughter worked at the restaurant on weekends. My husband asked that I focus my attention on bringing in new customers so I started visiting local businesses, introducing myself and our restaurant and handing out our menus. During my visits, I noticed that food was being delivered from area restaurants. I went back to our restaurant and told my son that we needed to cater. He told me that The Egg & I Restaurants didn't cater. I told him that if we wanted to keep our doors open and if corporate wanted their royalty check, we needed to cater. Remember, we were in survival mode at this point. He agreed and we began to offer catering. It helped sustain our business.

We also had **conversations** with our guests regularly. Several guests recommended that I visit networking groups to promote our restaurant. I took their advice and after a **conversation** with some like-minded networkers, soon realized that we could start a networking group in our restaurant's meeting room. The attendees would be exposed to our restaurant, purchase their lunch, and I could tell them about catering and our free meeting room. I also visited a local non-profit theater and had a **conversation** with their Director of Marketing and Development. I explained our situation and asked if they would be interested in giving us advertising opportunities in return for in-kind donations. He agreed and a beautiful relationship was formed.

In August, 2009, nine months later, it was determined that we were not at fault for the credit card fraud. The bank released most of the monies, minus some credit card penalties. It was a very tough time, but we had made it.

We were soon gifted with our second grandson and two years after opening our first restaurant, we opened our second restaurant in Carrollton/W. Plano, Texas. We opened our third restaurant in Denton, Texas and were awarded Franchisee of the Year. All of our hard work and perseverance had paid off. Life was good.

Fast forward a few years later and my husband and I found ourselves in a very precarious business situation. It proved to be catastrophic and put us in the worst possible situation of our lives. A business associate of mine, through many **conversations** on the jobsite, had told my husband and me about Tres Dias. He could see the stress we were under and the toll it was taking on both of us. Tres Dias is a weekend that encourages fellow Christians to grow closer to God, get more involved in their church and ultimately serve others. My husband attended the men's weekend first and came home a changed man. He was at total peace. I couldn't believe it.

I then attended the women's weekend. The **conversations** and talks throughout the weekend had given me hope again. By Sunday afternoon, I was laughing and back to my old self. I had decided to truly hand everything over to God. When I made that decision, I felt physically lighter. My husband and I are forever grateful for those serving on our weekends and for our friend inviting us. Both of us truly handed the situation over to God from that point on. We became more active in our church and began teaching 4 and 5 year-olds each Sunday. You cannot help but fall in love with each and every one of them. We became closer and even began to pray for the people causing us our pain. We have both served every Tres Dias weekend for the last two years and consider it an incredible privilege. Although my faith has always been strong, I am now reading the bible like never before. When I miss reading in the morning, I truly feel the difference throughout the day. My husband and I now have two incredibly good men that are helping us through this difficult situation. We have no doubt that God put them in our lives as it was through a **conversation** with a woman facilitating a neighborhood bible study that I found them. We could never have survived this ordeal or gotten this far without them. We are forever grateful.

In May, 2013 I had a feeling that something just was not right with my mother. She was avoiding my calls and that was not like her at all. I knew it was because she did not want me to worry about something. That was her way. She and I were extremely close and that feeling was confirmed that Mother's Day. The doctor had found a mass on her uterus. She would be going in for a CAT Scan that week to determine if it was malignant. I immediately flew up to New York but by the time I had landed, she had been rushed to the hospital in pain. It was a tumor and the cancer had spread throughout her body. Looking at her, she looked amazing. You would never know that something was wrong with her. Three days later, we were in a hospice room overlooking Central Park. It was surreal. Although it was the hardest, saddest time of my life... God blessed us all. My family was given the opportunity to love on my mother and have many **conversations** with her about our lives and how much we loved and appreciated her. God answered my prayers as he took her quickly, gently and without pain. Not a day goes by that I do not miss her but I am comforted to know that she has gone home to her heavenly father, and that she is reunited with her mother and son. I also know that I will be with her again someday.

Fast forward two years to July 2015, when during a self-exam I felt a lump. It was just 2 months after my yearly mammogram. I immediately wondered if it was residual from all the stress from that situation I mentioned and the death of my mother. I called a friend who had battled breast cancer twice. She was amazingly comforting and walked me through the process. I went in for a sonogram the following day and the doctor told me I would need a biopsy. Anyone who has experienced this knows that time stands still when you hear those words. Unfortunately, they were scheduling two months out. I prayed and prayed in my head as the doctor talked. I was leaving for vacation in two days and I would not be able to relax. Miraculously as the technician searched the computer, there was a cancellation and I could get in the following day. I only told my husband and my Tres Dias community so that they could pray for me. I did not want anyone else to worry unnecessarily. I worried, of course, about my children. There is a family history of breast and uterine cancer in my family, so there is a greater risk. During the time I waited for the results, I continued to pray and I kept asking myself if I had fulfilled my purpose here on earth? What if this is it? What do I need to do for my children to prepare them? I even thought that if I had breast cancer, thank God my mother wasn't alive as it would break her heart. I can't explain it but I just kept feeling as though I needed more time to help others. I kept feeling as though all the hard times were behind us and that God had something more planned for us. Either way, I decided during that time of waiting that I wanted nothing but joy in my life. That feeling of being at the beach. I knew that I did not want negative energy or people around me anymore causing stress and I wanted to help others. I also had to accept that it was all in God's hands. That Friday, while walking in Central Park, the nurse called and told me that the tumor was benign. I broke down crying and immediately thanked God. The experience truly put priorities and situations into perspective. Any woman who has experienced this knows that you walk around with a smile from ear to ear for weeks and truly look at life differently.

After returning from vacation, my husband and I had the privilege of serving with a non-profit organization called MetroRelief in feeding the homeless. I could not believe my eyes when we reached our destination in downtown Dallas. There was a tent city of homeless people. MetroRelief told us in preparation for the day, that we were not there just to feed people, we were there to have **conversations** and build relationships. The **conversations** we had with homeless folks that day changed us all. Our perceptions were shattered and we were all truly humbled. All I kept saying was, "I didn't get the memo. If I didn't get the memo then others did not get the memo either and we need to tell people about this so they can help." I was told to figure out what God given talents I could use to spread awareness. My husband immediately said radio or TV because I had done both and loved it. I told him it wasn't that easy. However, I prayed and thought back to the day in Central Park after I got the good news. Through a series of events that was clearly God's plan, I started hosting an Internet radio show. I named it, what else… **Hope Through Conversations**. On the show, I have **conversations** with non-profit organizations and individuals talking about various social issues, striving to make a difference, etc. in an effort to spread awareness, educate, prevent and promote involvement. There is also a **Hope Through Conversations** Facebook page which is used to further help spread awareness through social media.

I also serve on the Board of WaterTower Theatre (yes, that non-profit theater that gave us advertising in exchange for in-kind donations) and Chair their affinity group—Women of WaterTower. You never know where a **conversation** will take you!

Family, friends and business associates have urged me to write books about various personal and professional experiences for years. I attended a writing workshop this January in Florida facilitated by someone I respect and admire. It was held at the beach which is my happy place. As soon as I came over the bridge and saw the water…my shoulders went down 4 inches. The smell of the salt air made me smile. It was a time of reflection and clarity and great **conversations**. I met some incredible women during my stay and had time to write and figure out what was next for me in terms of my career and personal goals. One thing was clear…I want to try to always feel the way I do when I am at the beach. Calm, in-tune, happy and refreshed. I would also love to help others feel that way as well.

Outside the Fishbowl Looking In is my consulting business. I assess businesses from both a business owner's perspective and a customer's perspective and suggest changes to help increase sales. I also work with Women Entrepreneur's in helping them find life/work balance—that "beach" feeling.

I truly believe you build your business by building relationships so I attend many networking groups. I am continuously asked for recommendations for low-cost advertising by women entrepreneurs. One day I came up with the idea to host a radio show called WE Radio – Women Entrepreneur Radio. It is a show that is dedicated to a woman entrepreneur's business, product and/or service through **conversation**. They receive the MP3 of the show to use on their website and social media at an affordable price. It will not only help the women entrepreneur and her business, but it will help other women entrepreneurs with regards to best practices. I absolutely love working with like-minded women and have been asked for years to start an all-women's networking group or a MasterMind Group for Women Entrepreneurs. That too may be in my future. I also enjoy teaching people how to cook quick easy meals over tea or wine and of course, **conversation**! Maybe a show called Hope Through Wine, Cooking and **Conversations** may be in my future as well.

So what is my purpose? I have learned that I have many purposes. God has given me a passion for people and a voice that I believe He wants me to use to help and inspire others. For that I am thankful. I want to continue to try to make a positive difference in any way I can and with the people in my life and with anyone I meet. A simple hello and a small act of kindness can literally change their day and it doesn't cost you anything. Whatever the future holds for me, God shows me over and over again that He is in control and that I need to hand over my problems to follow HIS lead. I have also been shown over and over again that it is not an accident when people come into our lives and that there is always **Hope Through Conversation**! ▪

ROSE COLAROSSI. *When you meet Rose Colarossi, you soon see that Rose has never met a stranger! She will talk to anyone and she makes everyone she talks to feel as though they have known her forever. She is the one that approaches the person in the room who looks as though they are struggling and she introduces them to everyone. It is clear that she has a true passion for helping people and that she cares about everyone she meets. Rose has said many times over the years that we should all treat one another with the same level of respect and kindness that we would want someone to extend to our own parents, grandparents or children. She tells us all that each of us is here for a greater purpose and that we should strive to make a difference in this world one kind deed at a time.*

Rose is an accomplished entrepreneur, consultant and inspirational public speaker. She owned and operated a women's fitness center for almost ten years, and she and her family own three restaurants in North Dallas. She founded and hosts North Dallas Networking Group and founded and hosts two internet radio shows; **Hope Through Conversations**—*a show that focuses on social issues and WE Radio/Women Entrepreneur Radio, offering a low-cost means to advertise for women entrepreneurs. She serves on the Board at a non-profit theatre and chairs their Women's Group. Rose advocates and supports dozens of non-profits. She has co-authored a Behind Her Brand Entrepreneur Series and is currently writing several books. A finalist for the 2016 Female Entrepreneur Award presented by Addison Magazine for the most influential female entrepreneurs in North Dallas, Rose has touched the lives of many. Reach out to Rose to speak on inspirational, motivational and educational topics as it relates to both business and personal experiences as well as consulting services.*

Rose Colarossi
connect@rosecolarossi.com
972-824-5222

6

The Momepreneur Lifestyle Strategist
Denise Damijo

When I was first invited to be a part of *The Difference Maker Volume 6*, I was asked to tell my story. That was a little bit challenging for me because I view a story as having a beginning, middle, and end. As I took a look at my life, I began to realize that I am just starting the middle of my life. I'm really at the stage where I'm about to give birth in so many different ways. So, let me just give you a 30,000 foot view of my incomplete story.

It's funny because many people think that in order to become a difference maker in the world they would have to have an excellent foundation, great role models in their life, and be educated by the best so that they could become the best. At least that's what I thought. I looked at different difference makers and I thought to myself that they have had and will always have a life full of kettle corn, rainbows, and cotton candy, while my life was more like horse manure, splinters, and paper cuts. I began to think that being a difference maker was too far out of my reach.

The thing is that I wanted to be a difference maker and I didn't even know why. It seemed like I had challenges since I was born. My childhood was like a Russian roulette game. Sometimes I had a guardian and sometimes I didn't. My biological parents were not the best fit for parenthood. They weren't evil or wicked people. They were just not parent material. I found myself playing musical guardians a lot. I entered into the foster care system at the young age of about a year old. From all of the pictures and the little journal that my foster mother kept, it was a very warm and loving place. Unfortunately, that is not where I stayed.

My biological mother thought it was a good idea to take a go at parenting again. That phase lasted a couple of years. Throughout those years, I can't remember much until the horrid day that I was placed in emergency foster care because my mother decided to walk with me only in my underclothes and no shoes in the SNOW! At that point, she was obviously in no condition to take care of me. All that I wanted to do was to go home and bounce on my trampoline that was in the middle of our living room floor. Instead, the only highlight of that evening was that I was able to eat pancakes at 12 a.m. with a new family that I didn't know. I stayed there for a while but like I said before, it was just an emergency placement. I then was placed in another good home and I was grateful. I stayed at that place for a while until my paternal grandmother petitioned the court for me to come and live with her. I was then shipped a couple of states away where my grandmother met me in the airport holding a balloon, a smile, a little sass and a whole lot of class.

I absolutely loved her. She was an awesome woman! She was beautiful, smart, caring, nurturing, but above all of that, SHE WAS MINE!!!! I loved to feel like I belonged. I am not going to give you kittens and hot fudge Sunday's by telling you that I was not a handful because I was. But even with all of my issues, she was always kind and loving to me. Spending time with her and unconsciously learning from her was the highlight of my childhood and looking back, it was really one of the most profound times of my existence. Unfortunately, the environment of experiencing happiness and kindness didn't last. When I was 9, she had gotten ill to the point where she could no longer take care of me. I was very blessed to have spent four beautiful years with her, but devastated when all of it came to an end.

But I survived…

I was back into emergency foster care and this time, there were NO nice people. I was passed around to places that did not celebrate the color of my skin, were just in it for the money, and people who liked to prey on innocent little girls. I spent years as a victim. Even as all of the bad things were occurring in my life, I heard this familiar voice telling me that I was significant. The voice kept telling me that I was special and I was going to do something to help many people. The voice kept telling me to continue to be kind, loving, and to want to give something good to the world. Sometimes I just wanted to tell that voice to shove it where the sun didn't shine because I just knew that the voice was not experiencing the mess called my life that I was. The voice was surely not seeing and feeling the same things that I was seeing and feeling. To be honest, I really felt like that voice was being insensitive and uncompassionate.

But throughout all of the years, that voice kept me grounded and helped me to not harden my heart. I learned later on in my life that the beautiful voice I heard was truly music to my ears.

It would've actually been nice to say that when I turned 18, all of my problems went away and my fairy God Mother turned my existence into a beautiful life I loved. That definitely didn't happen. Over time, I finally accepted that I didn't have a fairy God Mother. I concluded that she either retired or died when it was my turn. All I knew was that I actually had to make this thing happen myself.

As an adult, I had no idea of what to do or where to start. I had already had my first child and was getting ready to have my second. Throughout the years after my grandmother got sick, I had no guidance, no one to help me learn how to become successful in life, and no one who I could express all of my concerns, fears, or even triumphs to. I was alone and I truly felt broken.

But I survived…

Reminiscing back to when I walked across the stage after I graduated with getting my A.S. degree in accounting, I remember hearing all of the other people that walked across the stage had their family and friends screaming and cheering them on. It was exciting and EXHILARATING! My name finally got called and I almost forgot that I wouldn't have that. After they called my name, I waited for someone to tell me good job or scream and make noises and sounds like I heard before. But instead, it was silent. You could almost hear a pin drop. I was embarrassed. On a day that was supposed to be exciting and that I was supposed to remember as a milestone in my life that I accomplished, it just became a day that I wanted to forget.

But I survived…

In my early 20s, I took on the responsibility of taking care of my father who started to show the same signs as my grandmother's debilitating disease. He had also become very forgetful and could no longer take care of himself. Even though he didn't do the same for me, I tried to do my best in taking care of him for four years until he had to get a permanent feeding tube placed in his stomach. By then he was in diapers, couldn't bathe himself, feed himself, and he was in a wheel chair. When they told me that it would be best for him to have round the clock nursing care, it hurt me but in the same breath it was a sigh of relief. I was only 24 years old, a mother of two, and I was EXHAUSTED.

I wanted something different. I needed something different. I didn't want to stay in the same place where all of those bad memories haunted me. I wanted and desperately needed a fresh start for me and my children.

I packed three suitcases, my children, and took a one-way flight from California to Houston, Texas.

I got off the plane not knowing how it was going to be in a new city, a new state and really depending on people who I didn't know to be as welcoming as I needed them to be.

I just wanted to finally fit in and be accepted. Unfortunately, I found myself in a very familiar circumstance, surrounded by people who didn't really care or love me, but just tolerated me and felt the need to purposely make me feel like the third wheel.

But I survived…

I came to realize that sometimes when your calling is great, you are never meant to fit into everyone's circle.

It was tough and sometimes I didn't believe that I could make it but I was determined. I was determined to do something greater than myself and greater than my current circumstances.

I struggled for years continuing my education to get my B.S degree in Business Management. I also struggled trying to raise two children while sometimes working two jobs and going to school full time. I got so accustomed to struggle that I no longer heard the voice that was constantly telling me that I was special and I had something great to give to the world.

One day, life had just gotten so stressful that I had to just sit and be still. I knew that something wasn't right. And I knew that there was more to life than what I was living at the time. Then the intervention came.

I was TIRED of just surviving!!!! I needed more! I was more than just a story of survival!!!!

The voice started speaking again. The voice was telling me that I was supposed to have my own business and not work for someone else. The voice told me that I would be able to help many people and that I needed to start building.

On the bright side, I was ecstatic to have the voice back! On the other hand, I believed that the voice had completely lost its mind. My own business? Help people? Start building????? The voice had completely gone mad! I couldn't even help myself. I was living paycheck to paycheck. I had no idea how to start a business or be a business owner, and I was completely clueless as to what I was supposed to start building.

It took me a couple of more years to even begin the journey of starting my own business. I just couldn't take that jump out of the boat. I hadn't decided to be all in. I barely had my pinky toe in. When I truly made the decision that I was ALL in, was when I put in my two-week notice and started a journey that was going to change and shape my life forever. Then I found out that I was pregnant! My husband and I had been trying for a while to no avail and right when I decided to quit my job and start my entrepreneurial journey was when my bundle of joy decided to come.

I still quit…I was determined to do more than just survive. I needed to live and not just exist. I had to follow my core desires and not shy away from them because there were challenges up ahead.

Some people may tell you that when they decided to quit their job and start their own business, it was the happiest day of their life. Well, I'm going to be honest with you and say I think they tell lies!!!!! I was completely terrified! I had so much doubt in my mind! I didn't even know how to legally start a business, or run a business, or who were even going to be my customers, AND I was pregnant!!! EVERYTHING was new to me and it was very scary and overwhelming.

The good thing was, I was willing to go through it because I was no longer settling for just survival. I was going to be living! I was moving towards my dreams instead of running from them. I was making the choice to be a part of the solution and to help others in the process.

I decided that everything that I didn't know, I would learn and that is exactly what I started to do. I started to learn. I legally created my business and I got mentors and coaches that would help develop and challenge me. I read books and took classes and workshops. I asked other business owners about their experiences and I definitely was creating my own.

It was absolutely **AMAZING** to be able to help people while being a business owner! I was able to show and help women to see that they **CAN** have it all. I was able to show them that they didn't have to sacrifice one part of their life for the other. I shared my belief that you can have balance in your life that would bring you the happiness that you craved.

I traveled and met new people. I was able to spend ample time with my children and husband, and help people! I had become The Momepreneur Lifestyle Strategist.

Then the unthinkable happened…I got *PREGNANT* for the second time! It wouldn't have been so terrifying and frustrating, if my new bouncing baby boy wasn't only 6 months old. Having a pulmonary embolism two weeks after having my beautiful bouncing baby boy frightened me, because I hadn't even completely healed from that. Despite all of that, I still believed that I could do it ALL. I could still make it all work!

Then I found out that I was pregnant with **TWINS**!!!!

Can someone please scream for me!!!! Please pinch me and take me out of this nightmare!!!!

I was so happy because that is exactly what my husband wanted BUT I really was hoping that his wish wouldn't come true. Not because twins are bad but how the heck was I supposed to raise twins and a baby that is only 14 months older while maintaining my marriage, my two older children's schedules, and my awesome business!!!! I helped people find their identity and now I felt like I was losing mine.

How was I going to recover?

How was I going to survive this?

How was my life going to not be full of chaos?

Why does God hate me so much?

If crying could create lakes and rivers, I had definitely created one of my own. I was truly hurt and angry about my situation.

The good news is that the one thing that I have learned time and time again is that there is always light at the end of the tunnel. You just have to keep on moving towards that light. At first, it may look dark and ugly but the more you move forward, the more you will start to see a light at the end.

I made up my mind that despite my current circumstances, I was going to keep moving forward. I was going to keep a positive attitude. I was going to write down all of my goals and proactively work towards them.

I have to be honest with you. Throughout my twin pregnancy, it was tough. I had wanted to throw in the towel many times, and I was exhausted most of the time, but I kept persevering through it all.

I worked on strengthening my marriage and keeping it spicy because after God, my marriage was my foundation. I spent quality time and invested in my children. I was able to watch my oldest child graduate a year ahead of her class and do community service in another country where she spent three quarters of a year before she came back to prepare to go to college. I was able to help my son with projects, spend quality time with him and see him get accepted into a global studies academy. I was able to teach my youngest his first words and see him walk for the first time. I had peace of mind knowing that I was doing what I was called to do.

I did webinars, guest spoke on webinars, interviewed people, spoke at my events and at places like women's conferences. I blogged and did YouTube videos. I created programs that would help other women get through the hard times and celebrate their victories. And now as you are reading my chapter, I have also become a published author. I decided to continue to speak to and help the many women who are struggling to find a way out of what seems to be no way, and *I love it!*

I was relentless…

Failure or defeat was not an option for me…I was going to win no matter what I faced!

In the process, I've learned that difference makers all have their own unique journey and story. They have decided to stand for and/or against something and despite everything else that could possibly go wrong, they have decided to **NEVER** give up. After all the things that they had to overcome, they have decided to give back to the world.

Now, in the beginning of the middle of my journey, I have a husband who loves and supports me, five children who are loved and treasured dearly, a life that I love, and a business that I am very proud of. I am blessed to be able to serve people by helping them overcome their chaos, find their identity, and actually follow the inner voice that we all have inside of us that tells us that there is more to our lives other than our current situation.

We all have had days, weeks, and sometimes years where it has been a constant struggle not to suffocate from the situations and circumstances that we found ourselves in. Getting through those rough times is imperative to our success in fulfilling our deepest desires. I know that I couldn't have done it alone. I was blessed to have people who helped me through all of my chaos throughout the different periods of my life, and God's powerful voice speaking life into mine.

In order to serve you while you are reading my story, I want to give you a few tips:

- Despite fear, doubt, and anxiety, start your journey towards your dreams.

- Don't wait until things are perfect to start because they will NEVER be.

- Always remember that you can and will figure things out.

- Always believe in yourself and your purpose.

- Never give in or give up

- Celebrate YOU

"Champions aren't made in the ring, they are merely recognized there."

~Joe Frazier~

DENISE DAMIJO *is the founder and CEO of Denise Damijo International, LLC. She is originally from California but she moved to Texas in order to create a fresh start for herself and her two children. Throughout the time that she has been in Texas, Denise has been able to persevere through many challenges and to build a business that she loves and that has touched many people. She is determined to help as many people as possible to find balance, identity, and hope in a busy and forever changing fast paced world. As The Momepreneur Lifestyle Strategist she loves doing webinars, blogging, and YouTube videos to reach and connect with the women who relate to her. She enjoys speaking at events and showing women how they can become empowered by using her proven strategies and practical applications to gain control of their life and business and start investing in their dreams.*

Denise is excited about continuing her journey in creating more tools, programs, and events, that will continue to help, empower, and cultivate women to become the best that they can be and to live the life that they love to live.

Connect with Denise Damijo today on Facebook, YouTube, Twitter, LinkedIn or any of the following places.

Denise Damijo
denisedamijo.com
denise@denisedamijo.com

7

Staying Focused
Peggy Gaines

Peggy, a long-time happily married mother of two, had her life in balance. She had learned meditation and used it to help her relax and to sleep soundly. Life was good, until one day when her son Nathan was 17 years old, they learned he had a malignant brain tumor. Peggy relied on meditation to stay calm and focused as she and her husband navigated their son's care. Meditation saved Peggy—and now her mission in life is to help everyone learn and use this incredible tool.

"I think I have a brain tumor," my 17 year old son said to me. I wanted to refute him but the odd thing was, that exact thought had mysteriously entered my mind only moments before he said it.

We had just returned from an idyllic family vacation to Glacier National Park in Montana. Our days had been filled with fresh air, hiking and sunshine. We had climbed the path to Iceberg Lake, a place so spectacularly beautiful that I told my kids, Nathan and Heather, "This is where God lives."

Nathan was the picture of health; he exercised, lifted weights and ate right. He was a bright, funny and kind young man, ready to begin his senior year in high school. On the Montana trip, he had tried to write a postcard to his girlfriend but told his sister he had trouble forming the letters. I brushed it off as a symptom of hypochondria, a male dominant trait passed down from his father. I told him he probably had pinched a nerve when he was lifting weights. If it was still a problem when we got home, we would go to a chiropractor. There were no headaches, no seizures and no typical signs that something was wrong.

Long story short, it was a brain tumor. If you are a parent, you know there is little worse in life than finding out that your child is facing a life-threatening illness.

The demands of motherhood were ramping up to levels that I had never anticipated. My husband worked to find the most promising treatment, the top hospitals and the best doctors, but I was on the front lines. I needed to make all the appointments, drive to all the doctors' offices and hospitals, keep track of the meditations, comfort and care for my sick child and most importantly, be the head cheerleader, always keeping a positive outlook. What I really wanted to do was crawl back into bed and pull the sheets up over my head. But that was not an option. I needed something to help me cope with this terrifying situation.

Fortunately, I had what I needed—meditation. I always had a good relationship with God and I certainly leaned on Him now. But the tool that I used to augment that relationship was meditation. It gave me an inner strength that literally kept me breathing through this ordeal.

I began meditating about 6 years earlier because, like so many people, I was having trouble falling asleep. I bought a book on meditation, began listening to some cassette tapes and went to a class or two. Pretty soon I was meditating 20 minutes daily. My sleep improved dramatically and life was perfect—or at least I thought it was at the time.

With my son's diagnosis, life changed dramatically. I stopped working and focused on getting my son the help that he needed. Nathan had surgery and began treatment, which included traveling from our home in Florida to Duke Medical Center in North Carolina. I meditated everywhere; in every plane, waiting room and exam room. I taught Nathan how to meditate and he did it when he was getting radiation, chemotherapy and multiple MRIs.

This continued for about three years and then…the brain tumor got the better of him. It was time to help my son prepare to die.

My biggest concern during his time in hospice was that he not be afraid, so we talked about EVERYTHING. When the time came for him to cross over, I was very sad but I was not depressed. I had never felt angry or alone during the ordeal. I knew that we were supported by something bigger than ourselves every step of the way. Instead of thinking that this was the worst thing that could ever happen to our family, I thought,"I am so grateful Nathan was part of our life for 20 years. I'm so grateful that I got to be his mother."I knew I had been given the gift of a tool that everyone needed to know about.

Everyone has events in their life that can seem to be too difficult to handle. It may be an overwhelming number of little things that add up until you just cannot take it anymore or it may be one crushing blow that stops you in your tracks. Whatever it is, you can handle it when you have the peace and inner strength that you find when you take time to be still and meditate.

There isn't a day that goes by that I don't think of my son. I honestly feel that I was chosen to go through that experience so that I could teach others this important practice. Meditation is a life skill that everyone needs to know.

As a society, we have become consumed with the external worries and trappings of life. We are always connected to something or someone else with our cell phone and computer.

Our eyes are constantly focused downward as we check the texts, apps, and contacts from sites and people we may have little real connection with. Meanwhile, the true essence of life is passing us by. We don't look up long enough to notice the sky; we have no idea if the day is sunny or cloudy. We only notice the weather when it interferes with our comfort. As we walk to our car with our head scanning our iPhone, we miss the cool breeze that brushes our cheek. We can't remember the last time we heard a bird singing or noticed the phase of the moon. When was the last time that we looked up at the night sky, simply to admire the stars? Instead of noticing the gifts the universe is giving us, we focus on our never-ending list of things to do. We ruminate about yesterday and worry about tomorrow, all while forgetting to"live"today.

We've lost our soul and our true connection with ourselves. We feel alone, unsupported by the universe. Its"you and me against the world". And conventional wisdom tells us the world is a scary place. Therefore, you feel as though you always need to be on guard, always on alert. You live in a constant state of fight or flight, ready to defend yourself or run for cover at a moment's notice. No wonder you feel panicked. We believe the world is out of control.

The truth is, life is unpredictable and sometimes incredibly tough to handle, but the universe has not abandoned you. We are not on our own.

With meditation you learn to find calm and inner strength. You feel a true connection with the Source. You know that no matter how difficult life may become, you will have the inner peace that comes from a peace not of this world. It is a knowing that you are loved and supported by something greater than yourself and you are never alone.

One way to find that inner peace, the inner calm and stillness that's missing from our life, is with meditation.

Is there Proof that Meditation Works?

People have been meditating more than 3000 years in the East but it's fairly new to the Western world. In the early 1970s, Herbert Benson, a Harvard physician, began studying stress-related illnesses and noted that it seemed to be a phenomenon of the West.[1] When they looked at the East, in countries such as India with its stressful environment of poverty and overcrowding, they found that the population did not have the same health problems. Researchers hypothesized that it was due to the prevalence of meditation.

Now, 45 years later, there is a plethora of studies showing that meditation actually changes the brain. A group of Harvard affiliated re-searchers at Massachusetts General Hospital found that within 8 weeks of meditative practice, there was measurable change in the amygdala or fight and flight center of the brain. [2]http://blogs.scientificamerican.com/guest-blog/what-does-mindfulness-meditation-do-to-your-brain/

With meditation, you will still worry and still lose your temper, but the way that you will begin to look at things will begin to change. I realized that is what happened to me with my son. I was able to look at life differently. When I looked at the situation instead of feeling that my son's death was the worst thing that could ever have happened, I thought I was so glad that Nathan had been part of our family for 20 years. I was so grateful I had been chosen to be his mother. Instead of focusing on what we had lost, I focused on the gift we had been given. I was able to do this because my brain had changed and so had my perspective on life.

How Does Meditation Work?

When we are stressed, we go into the fight and flight state. In this state, our breathing is shallow, our heart rate increases and our blood pressure goes up.

The fight and flight state is a protective response that was helpful when we were cave men and were being chased by saber-toothed tigers. While we were escaping, we were in the fight and flight state but once we got away from the tiger we were able to relax. Our heart rate slowed down, our breathing became deeper and our blood pressure returned to normal.

The problem is, today we live in the fight and flight state. We've forgotten how to return to the relaxed state. We live in a constant state of alertness. "What's that sound? What's going on? I've got to remember this; I can't forget that!"

That's the way we live, but our bodies weren't created to live constantly in this state. As a result, we begin to manifest signs of stress. We begin having headaches, neck and back pain; grind our teeth at night, have trouble sleeping, suffer from indigestion, and high blood pressure. Our tempers are short, we stress, eat, drink and numb our feelings with medication.

This constant level of stress is killing us. But we can do something about it.

The Magic Key

The magic key to relieving the stress and getting out of the 'fight and flight state' is becoming aware of our breath. When we are in the 'fight and flight state' we breathe shallow and we only use the top part of our lungs. But our lungs go to the bottom of our rib cage. We are designed to breathe with our full lungs; that's why they are there.

Why this Works

As you probably remember from high school biology, the diaphragm is a dome-shaped muscle that separates our lungs from our abdominal cavity. When we breathe shallow (which is what we do in the fight and flight state) the diaphragm just sits there and nothing happens. But when we breathe with our full lungs, the full lungs put pressure on the dome shaped diaphragm causing the diaphragm to flatten out. When we exhale, the diaphragm returns to its dome shape, when we inhale it flattens out again. This is significant because there is a nerve that innervates the diaphragm, called the vagus nerve. When the diaphragm moves up and down with our breath, the vagus nerve is stimulated and it sends the message to the brain to "Relax".

Breathing with our full lungs, diaphragmatically, is the way we are supposed to be breathing all the time. However, right now we are mindful of the way we are breathing only while we meditate. As we become mindful of the way we are breathing, eventually diaphragmatic breathing will become a habit so that we breathe this way all the time and not just when we are meditating.

Try this exercise

Sit up straight, with your head, neck and spine in alignment. Put your feet flat on the floor. Place your hands on your ribcage. As you breathe in through your nostrils, breathe just a little deeper than you normally breathe. Don't breathe as though you are trying to blow up a balloon. Just breathe a little deeper and feel your ribs expand as you breathe in. Notice how your ribs contract as you exhale. Breathe in again and feel your ribs expand; feel your ribs contract as you exhale.

Now put your hands in your lap. Allow your eyes to close and relax your shoulders. Breathe in again and be mindful of your ribs expanding as you inhale and contract as you exhale. Continue breathing in and breathing out. As you breathe in, take your awareness to the tip of your nose. Notice the cool air as you breathe in and your ribs expand. Notice how the air is warm as you exhale and your ribs contract.

You can think to yourself: "I am breathing in, I am breathing out. Cool air in; warm air out. I am breathing in; I am breathing out." This is a brief meditation. Try it for 2 minutes and then notice how you feel. You will find that you are feeling calmer, more relaxed and focused.

Myths about meditation

As a nurse, I get referrals from cardiologists, internists and psychologists to teach their patients meditation. When people come to me for instruction, the most common statement is "I can't meditate, I have too many thoughts."

The fact is, everybody has too many thoughts. Everybody is bouncing from one thought to the next. But research has found that a wandering mind is often an unhappier mind because our mind often focuses on worries and concerns. [3]http://greatergood.berkeley.edu/article/item/how_to_focus_a_wandering_mind

There are many myths about meditation. A couple of the myths include the mistaken idea that meditation is about mind control or that meditation is about stopping your thoughts or blanking out your mind. All of these ideas are wrong.

Its impossible to stop your mind from thinking and meditation has no intention of doing such a thing. Meditation is exercise for your brain. When you are meditating and your thoughts wander, you will notice what has happened and you simply bring your awareness back to your breath. You will repeat that over and over again. This action of noticing that your mind has wandered off and refocusing your awareness on your breath is like a bicep curl for your brain. As your mind wanders off and you guide it gently back to your breath, you are actually training your brain to stay focused and on task. Researchers have found when distracted, the person who meditates is able to refocus faster than the person who doesn't meditate. [4]http://lifehacker.com/what-happens-to-the-brain-when-you-meditate-and-how-it-1202533314

If you feel that you would like to experience the power and benefits of meditation, I have multiple programs—both virtual and in person—that can help you develop a practice. Simply call or email me through my website www.MeditationWithPeggyGaines.com to set up a session to discuss if and how my programs can support you in decreasing stress and increasing your enjoyment of everything that life has to offer. ▪

[1] The Relaxation Response Herbert Benson, MD Harper tech 1975

[2] http://blogs.scientificamerican.com/guest-blog/what-does-mindfulness-meditation-do-to-your-brain/

[3] http://greatergood.berkeley.edu/article/item/how_to_focus_a_wandering_mind

[4] http://lifehacker.com/what-happens-to-the-brain-when-you-meditate-and-how-it-

PEGGY GAINES, *RN, BSN is a nurse educator and is nationally board certified as a Clinical Meditation Specialist. She has been meditating for over 18 years She has first-hand knowledge of the positive impact that meditation can have in one's life.*

Peggy is married and the mother of two children, Nathan and Heather. When their son Nathan was 17 years old, he developed a malignant brain tumor. Peggy relied on meditation to help her stay calm and focused as she and her husband navigated the care of their son.

Everybody can benefit from knowing skills and techniques that can be used when life gets tough. Meditation is such a tool. Peggy teaches meditation classes for individuals and corporations.

She lives in Coconut Grove, Florida with Michael, her husband of 31 years.

Peggy Gaines
gainespeggy@gmail.com
MeditationwithPeggyGaines.com
305-609-4433

8

Blue-Collar Proud:
Raising the Standard, Changing the World
Taylor Hill and Carter Harkins

This is about our mission, to stand proudly with Blue Collar business owners and tradesmen who start and run excellent service businesses. It's about what we have learned through the years of partnering with them. We are honored and privileged to serve the people that serve the world. We are Blue-Collar Proud.

> "People value you to the exact degree that you value yourself."
>
> ~Anonymous

Roger was on his knees with a flashlight and shining it up into the dark interior of a large fireplace. He was peering with expert eyes into the chimney in order to discover the source of the problem his customer had called about. He couldn't remember how long he had been looking up there, but suddenly he became aware of voices behind him. He listened as the homeowner, a physician, led his son into the room, saying to him, "Come here son, I think it's important for you to see this. You see what kind of dirty work this man has to do every day? If you don't go to college and get your degree, this is what you'll end up doing for the rest of your life."

When our client first told us this story about one of his employees, it brought tears to our eyes. First, because this very successful business owner and his employees had been devalued by another human being. This customer needed them to perform a specialized service that he was unable to do for himself! Second, because it isn't the first time we have heard stories like this. In a world that has very specific ideas about what success looks like, it is very apparent that honest, hard-working blue-collar tradesmen and women do not meet the standard.

Why is that? How could it be that we would look down upon someone who is willing to train themselves in specialized knowledge that solves the world's very real problems?

For years, we have had the privilege of working with clients who are the owners of blue-collar service businesses all over the country. We have long been focused on providing top-notch, done-for-you marketing services for growth, but we came to realize that the needs were far greater than just marketing. As we now see it, this is an opportunity to change the world.

Does it sound preposterous to you to utter words like "blue-collar" and "world changing" in the same breath? The way we see it, when a business owner doesn't value what he does for the world, it affects every aspect of his life and his community. It impacts the way he will treat his employees. It will be subtly communicated in every marketing message and every customer interaction. This lack of value and respect will stare back at him in the mirror every morning, and reinforce the persistent stereotypes surrounding blue-collar skilled trades in every industry.

If you don't treat yourself with respect, why should anyone else?

But what would the world look like if blue-collar business owners were serious about creating the kinds of businesses that were respected in their community? What if these businesses were perceived as among the most desirable places to work, where leadership and opportunity were found in abundance? Where community service was held as a prime value that motivated every single thing they did? How differently would these business owners treat their customers if they truly understood the value of what they do? How would the world's perception and estimation change when thinking of hard, dirty, blue-collar skilled trades and business ownership?

Did you know that in 2014, approximately 11 million people in the US were unemployed? At the same time, there were over 7 million blue-collar jobs that went unfilled. These were jobs doing the essential work of building and repairing the infrastructure of our roads, bridges, and dams. These jobs served the everyday needs of our buildings, homes, cars, etc. 11 million people needed jobs, and 7 million jobs went unfilled. This disconnect is affecting many lives, and it's all because the work is considered unworthy, and beneath the status of a college educated citizen.

Our work is expanding beyond just being a marketing services provider. In 2016, we launched The Guys In Trucks Show. It's a weekly podcast with the mission of encouraging, educating and mentoring blue-collar business owners who see what they do as a real calling. Our listeners want to intentionally create the kinds of businesses that exemplify what it means to be Blue-Collar Proud.

More than just a show, Guys In Trucks is growing a community. We strive to be the conduit for real change in industries like Plumbing, Electrical, HVAC, Construction, Contracting, Chimney & Masonry, Handyman Services, Pest Control, Pool Maintenance, Janitorial, Landscaping, and many others.

We are championing what it means to be Blue-Collar Proud. We are challenging business owners and consumers alike to reconsider what it means to be in the skilled trades and home services. This is an $800 billion sector of our economy. With every story we find and share about amazing customer service, we also find stories about exceptional leadership, community building, compassion, humility, and integrity. We are changing the common perception of these amazing individuals that have aspired to the service of other human beings in need. Blue-collar service is not a fall-back career or business choice; it's a high calling, and one that only certain kinds of rugged, caring, committed people could ever hope to do.

We think the seeds of far-reaching change are present in the work we are doing now. Remember Roger, the chimney technician in the large home of a successful physician? When he heard the disparaging words spoken to his back that day, he stood up, turned around, and with patience and dignity replied, "You don't know me. You'll probably never be able to imagine why I do what I do, but the fact is that I CHOSE this work. I have a college degree. I love my family and am grateful that what I do is able to provide a good living for them. I love what I do because I get to serve people, just like you do in your medical office. I do not think that what I do is any less valuable to the world than what you do. I would hope you would want your son to be proud of what he does, whatever he decides to do."

This is our mission, to stand proudly with Roger and the business owners who start and run excellent service businesses. We are honored and privileged to serve the people that serve the world. This is what it means to be Blue-Collar Proud.

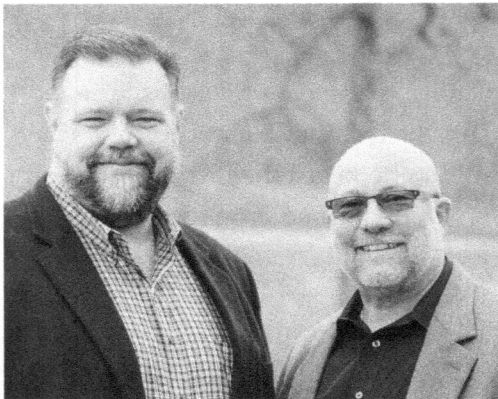

TAYLOR HILL
CARTER HARKINS

Business partners Taylor Hill and Carter Harkins are a duo that are rarely still nor separate. Whether they're managing the day-to-day activities of their digital marketing company, Spark Marketer, adding some finishing touches to one of their upcoming books Customer Service Marketing for Blue Collar Service Businesses *or* Crap My Dogs Taught Me About Business & Leadership, *speaking and sharing at a national convention or expo, or wrapping up another episode of their newly launched blue collar podcast Guys In Trucks, these two are serious about encouraging, inspiring, and serving the guys and gals that serve the world.*

Taylor Hill
Carter Harkins
guys@guysintrucks.com
guysintrucks.com
855-646-3538

9

You Made the Mess, Now Clean It Up and Shine Bright

Sheldon Horowitz

The room was dark, the spotlights were shining bright and it was time to party on this fine Saturday night. My favorite song, "2 of Amerikaz Most Wanted" by 2Pac and Snoop Dogg just started to play, meaning that the next four minutes were going to be one of the highlights of the night. Out to dance floor with my drink in hand, it was time to live the life of a boss, even if only vicariously through the lyrics that flowed so smoothly from the speakers above. As quick as the song began, only moments later it was fading into the background as the next song that made the crowd go wild was taking over. Moments quickly turned into hours, hours into long nights, weeks and months. In the blink of an eye, the 18-month whirlwind that was my early twenties came to a screeching halt when the iron bars of Long Beach County jail were closing behind me at three o'clock on that fateful Sunday morning.

How long am I going to be stuck in this place? Where do I sleep since there are 18 other people in this cell and only 8 metal planks that represent beds? How do I let the girls I am talking to know where to find me? The proverbial "Rock Bottom" that I had heard of so many times in the past seemed to be taking the form of the ice cold cement floor in this cell, also known as my bed for the first couple of nights. The next morning is when it hit me like a ton of bricks since we had to wake up and be done with breakfast by 6 am. In my world, that part of the day is considered the tail end of yesterday, not when I would have my first meal of the day completed. As it turned out, my stint in jail only lasted a little over 10,000 minutes—which translated into one week.

When asked to write this chapter of "Dare to be a Difference Maker", one particular quote initially came to mind.

"Insanity: doing the same thing over and over again and expecting different results"– Albert Einstein.

One of the purposes of this chapter is to share as candidly as possible, with the hope of being a part of the testimony of those who read, share and use this story as inspiration for their own growth. The next portion of this chapter is going to be dedicated to the back story and the set of circumstances that allowed me to learn and grow so much over time. Whether you can relate to some or all of the details and situations —or not a single one, I hope that you keep an open mind since the concepts can be applied to many different challenges in life.

• • •

As I mentioned earlier, it all started about 18 months before Long Beach jail welcomed me as their guest. Like most 21 year olds, I was pretty lost as to how to be an adult, and do adult things. Having already dropped out of college and with about one year under my belt as a slightly above minimum wage office worker, I had given up hope on ever achieving many of the adult type goals that I had heard so much about growing up. In order to save up enough money for a down payment on a house, would take four years of saving every penny that I earned to come up with that much money. Since I used 100% or more of each paycheck I received simply to pay rent, eat and take the bus to and from work, I quickly realized that the American Dream wasn't meant for me, unless of course I could hit it big somehow. The most logical way I could figure out was to be a semi-professional poker player when I wasn't working during the day. What this entailed was taking two hours' worth of bus rides after work to the local casino, losing whatever money I had, then taking the two hour bus ride of shame back home. Needless to say, my get-rich-quick scheme didn't pan out so well for me since what little extra money I had at the time would always be lost at the poker tables. This continued for about six months and as time went on, the trips to the casino were more of an adrenaline rush than an actual plan to make enough extra money to improve the quality of my life.

If going to the casino once or twice a week was fun and enjoyable, gambling on sports consistently and figuring out how to gamble even more would only add to the rush! As tends to be the case, my lack of a consistent sleeping schedule started to affect how I performed at work, which assured that my income and position at the company would not advance in the right direction. Since additional gambling would require more funds, I had to be creative in securing the means necessary to feed the gambling beast within. At this point, my decision was to take the path of least effort, in spite of my morals. As a result, stealing money from the company where I worked seemed like a pretty feasible option. The first time was the toughest as the sick feeling in my stomach was unmistakable. I will definitely pay this money back with interest since the gambling tides are due to turn in my favor. Of course, they didn't and once again the money in my wallet helped to pay for the lights and air conditioning the casino provided to all of us. This time though the money wasn't really mine, yet it was gone just the same. One thing led to another, and six months later, I was fired for stealing money a minimum of two to four times per week.

At that point, I had no place to stay, no car to drive and really no one who wanted me around. So I did what anyone else in my position would do. I took my last paycheck and rented a car for the weekend so that I could figure things out. Behind the wheel of that new rental car I felt free, since I could drive wherever I wanted and do whatever I wanted on my own schedule. Since I already had a taste of being homeless and living in my car, the next step was to find someone to let me live with them. This turned out to be pretty easy as long as I kept my standard of living pretty low. During this next six months, I worked for less than a total of seven days, with the sole purpose of being able to buy a new shirt to go out in once per week. Even though productivity wasn't my strong suit during these times, there would always be enough money around to smoke some weed and drink some drinks. Kind of funny how that works! Remember that rental car that I took out for the first weekend? It was such a nice car, the idea of returning it was just too painful of a thought, so it stayed with me instead. That car was my pride and joy until six police cars pulled me over at 2:00 am on a Sunday morning and with guns drawn they let me know that they needed the car back. Grand Theft Auto was the charge, and that big jail cell was going to be home for the foreseeable future. Would I be in there for a few months, a couple of years or even longer?

For whatever reason, the rental car company decided not to press charges which meant that I only spent a week in jail. One of those days happened to be my 23rd birthday, which by the way, jail is a miserable place to turn a year older. My birthday cake that year was made from a mixture of soaked top ramen noodles, oatmeal and crushed up graham crackers. That was a joke, since there was no cake and the only person to mention it was my birthday was an employee who saw it on my record when I was being transferred to another area. Having no legitimate birthday wishes sent your way is worse than my imaginary cake would have tasted.

As you can see, my choices led to a couple of years of excessive gambling, stealing, drinking, drugs, lying, damaged relationships, and stealing some more. If you are still reading at this point you might be thinking—how does all of this make you a Difference Maker? If I wanted to hear a story of shenanigans and bad choices, there are plenty of movies I could be watching that are much more worthy of my time.

At this point, my goal is to share some key concepts, actions and beliefs that have allowed me to transform from the person in the story to who I am today. Whether or not any part of the story of my past is relatable to you, it is with high hopes that you will be able to take some of these ideas and pearls of wisdom that have been given to me, and use them to change yourself and the world around you.

"Work harder on yourself than you do on your job" – Jim Rohn.

Living by this concept is easy to do and even easier not to do. How do you work on yourself harder than your job, you might ask? Listen or read positive material each and every day. Thirty minutes or more per day will give you amazing results. However, starting and developing the habit is the most important part. Invest your resources (time, energy or money) into your continued education, whether it is attending a seminar, learning a new career or gaining skills in your current industry.

"You can't fly with eagles, when you keep walking with turkeys" – Unknown.

The day that you decide to change your way of thinking and beliefs about yourself, is the day you will notice a change in the attitudes of your circle of friends. The interesting thing about this change is that the only thing that is different today is your beliefs; your friends are the exactly the same as they were yesterday. We are like chameleons in that we adapt to our surroundings and the attitudes and beliefs that are around us. People who are at where you want to be in life think differently than you do. It is contagious if you allow yourself to be close enough.

"It is amazing what you can accomplish when you don't care who gets the credit" – Harry S. Truman.

If there is one quote that is worth making part of your philosophy, it is this gem. Whether it is in a relationship with family, friends, coworkers or your boss, everyone has an instinctive need to feel important and valuable. By choosing to incorporate these 15 words into your attitude about relationships, you will find that you will become a magnet to the people and tools necessary to fulfill your dreams.

I hope that you have enjoyed this chapter and that you have been able to grow from different aspects of it. Since we all love a happy ending, in the 10 years since my 23rd birthday, I have been fortunate enough to repay my debts as well as regain and create amazing relationships with my family and many new friends. Since my first personal development seminar in September 2007, I have attended over a dozen different events around the country and have met thousands of like-minded people. In my career, I have been able to help and mentor over a few dozen people from all different walks of life, deliver my own group-style seminars and be part of giving countless people the same opportunity I was given. After a long relationship, I recently married my loving wife Miranda and became a family with her and our 10-year-old daughter Maliyah. We all live together in the house we are fortunate enough to own. Since dreams do come true, every time I exercise at the gym, I make sure to play "2 of Amerikaz Most Wanted" in my headphones with a big smile inside.

SHELDON HOROWITZ. *Sheldon was raised by his parents Mitchell and Mary Jane in Los Angeles, California; and grew up with his younger brother Ryan. His favorite activities are taking his daughter Maliyah to ice skating, going on long car rides with his wife Miranda, and bowling with his father and brother. He started bowling at the age of 8 and began competitive tournaments a few years later; rolling his first perfect game at the age of 14. He has achieved the feat 15 times since. He began his career with Coast to Coast Computer Products at the age of 23 as a sales assistant and in his 10 years with the company, has grown into the role of a sales team leader. His first personal development experience was attending a Jim Rohn Seminar at the age of 24, and he has since participated in over a dozen events with an emphasis on goal setting, sales mastery, memory improvement, life coaching and much more. Being able to watch the people he has mentored become mentors and coaches to others are among his proudest accomplishments. In 2014, he became a Ziglar Legacy Certified instructor allowing him to pass on the timeless teachings to many more people.*

Sheldon Horowitz
sheldon@sheldonhorowitz.net
www.sheldonhorowitz.net
888-488-8830

10

Why Happiness is NOT a choice
(And 10 thoughts on living a happier life)

Maria Gabriela Jovel

Growing up in one of the poorest and most violent countries in the midst of a civil war, I learned as a kid that in every conflict, you are either part of the problem or part of the solution, and that you can either waste your energy complaining about what is wrong, or invest it in doing something about it. As a kid, I decided to invest mine spreading positive messages through music; but when I grew up, I got busy and distracted. It was again in the midst of chaos and pain, that I understood that happiness is our main duty as human beings, because if you are not a happy person, most likely you are making someone else miserable.

"Mom, you should smile more", my 7-year-old son said casually one day while playing with his Legos. He had no idea of how that phrase shook me to my core. I had always considered myself to be a happy person; so his words came like a bucket of ice thrown right at me. It was true that I had not been exercising the muscles of my face very often, at least not at home.

In my defense, I thought, who has the energy to run a company, be a wife, volunteer as a homeroom mom, be the CEO, CFO, and COO of a household, serve in the community and still walk around playing Miss Congeniality?

Excuses aside, in the bottom of my heart, I knew my son was right. After all, I had left my corporate job many years ago to focus on my dream of having a family. I had built my own company under the premise of pursuing life fulfillment and helping others "achieve their business goals while awarding them with the gift of time to do what they love". The truth is, I got lost on the way and even though I had a blessed life, I was focused on DOING and not on BEING.

About a year earlier, I had a wakeup call when I was diagnosed with a severe anemia and vitamin D deficiency; the latter was a clear sign of poor self-care, considering that one of the causes of this deficiency is lack of sunlight and I live three blocks away from the beach! Even though this health challenge affected me enough to decide to slow down, it wasn't what really made me stop and refocus.

A few months after I recovered from my condition, I received a second wakeup call. This time it was loud and clear. On the way back from a family vacation my son started complaining of stomach pain. He was treated for a stomach virus and Mesenteric Adenitis and rushed to the hospital a couple of times. Ten days later, he had arthritis and small hemorrhages in his legs, which completed the chart for the diagnosis of an autoimmune disease called Henoch–Schönlein Purpura (HSP). Seeing my little kid suffering and dealing with the uncertainty and possibility of the worst case scenarios, is something my husband and I would not have been able to endure without faith and the prayers and support from family and friends.

The world stopped for me during the days we were with him in the hospital and during his recovery period. Nothing mattered more than helping him get better and keeping the family together and strong. F ortunately, I could count on the support of a great team that kept my company going, and it was this experience what helped me get perspective and realize that I had been distracted. I understood that life is too short to be distracted, that our time in this earth is too precious to waste it being unhappy.

My heart was full of gratitude and a burning desire of sharing this realization. I started researching the topic of happiness and was fascinated with the amount of scientific proof that shows how success is a consequence of happiness and not the other way around. There was no going back, I decided to become the CHO (Chief Happiness Officer) of my house and my company from there on.

Many people think happiness is a choice. I used to be one of them, but not anymore. Let's take away the romanticism around the concept for a little while and consider this thought:

Happiness is NOT a choice, it's a Duty.

I know it sounds a bit radical, but bear with me for a minute so I can explain myself…

While it's true that happiness is a choice we make every day, its transcendental importance beyond ourselves makes it much more than an option that we can decide to take some days, most days, when we feel like it. It's an option we MUST take every day, for our own good, and the good of others. Here is why:

If you are not a happy person, most likely you are making someone else miserable, and it usually tends to be the people that is closer to you, the people that you love the most.

Think of the times when you've been cranky, sour, or just plain unhappy. Can you honestly say that your behavior or your state of mind has had no influence whatsoever on the people around you?

I know with certainty that when I'm not a happy camper, my house resembles a madhouse. As women, we have a special ability to influence the mood of the people around us. The truth is, if you are not happy, your unhappiness has an impact on at least one other person. So if you think about it, by striving for happiness, you are kind of doing a favor to the people around you. It's not selfish to focus on your own happiness. It's actually a duty that will have a positive impact on the world.

If we want a better world, a happier one, we need to take seriously the responsibility of not only choosing happiness every day in spite of our circumstances, but also to fulfill our duty of being happy to make up for the many unhappy people on our planet. Are we part of the group of people who is making happiness its duty, or are we part of the group that is contributing to the mess?

I. Pick a side

We need to pick a side. This is something I understood when I was a kid. I had the privilege of growing up in one of the smallest, poorest, and most violent countries in the world. It is a place of hard working people whose enthusiasm in the midst of calamity is almost absurd. There is a lack of resources that is compensated for with creativity. You can often see 30 people crammed in the back of a pickup easily making space for 5 more. It is a place where kids' lack of toys is compensated for with their imagination. They are capable of turning a volcanic rock or a plastic bottle into a soccer ball. It's a place where no war, poverty or natural disaster is able to break the spirit of its people, my beloved El Salvador.

[Happy thought #1: Happiness can be found in the most unexpected places, where you would think there is nothing people can celebrate, they celebrate being alive.]

I had a blessed childhood. Aside from a chubby figure that made me feel less-than-pretty and a bossy temper that often got me in trouble, my life as a kid was good. Being the second girl of four children, I never felt I was something special, except for my awesome and numerous family who met religiously every Sunday at my grandparents' house and made me feel that I was part of something great.

[Happy thought #2: Happiness has very little to do with WHAT you have and a lot to do with WHO you have in your life.]

I always had the feeling I lived in a magic bubble, but one day I started to pay attention to the news and realized that what was going on outside was not pretty. The country was in a civil war that had lasted almost 10 years by then, and things were not getting better. There were car-bombs in public places, government curfews, shootings on the streets and helicopter sounds at night were not unusual. We got used to those things being part of our lives and carried on with our normal activities. It is funny how today, I still cannot sit with my back towards the door in a restaurant. This is because we were told that we should always face the entrance in case of a shooting. In spite of all this, in some way I always knew I was going to be OK.

[Happy thought #3: Happiness is knowing you will be OK in the middle of the storm.]

As in any war, each side had its own version of the truth. The right and left were defending their beliefs and it was all very confusing to me, as I'm sure it was to half of the people putting their life on the line for this war. There was just one thing that I knew for sure. I had to do something about it. I could not watch with my arms crossed and not try to make things better.

II. Become part of the solution

Therefore, I grabbed a weapon. It was a state of the art and very powerful one. It was an Ibanez guitar that belonged to my father and that I used in my not-so-often guitar classes, where I learned the only 4 chords that I could play fairly well. I figured that no one would want to listen to what a teenager had to say. However, maybe, just maybe, someone would be willing to hear me sing. So with those 4 chords, I wrote a Christmas song about forgiveness and hope. My dad helped me get it recorded in a studio and distributed to the main radio stations in the country. Even though it didn't make it to the Grammys, it did make people smile, and I felt I had made a contribution to hope and healing towards the end of the armed conflict.

[Happy thought #4: Happiness has to do with knowing what your unique contribution to this world is.]

During the next couple of years, I used and abused those same 4 chords to write a couple more songs: one for the kids on the streets that was used internationally by UNICEF. There was another one about the pain that was caused by the war, which took me to a singing contest in Spain called OTI (I recently learned through Wikipedia that a girl named Shakira was supposed to be in that contest on the same year, go figure!). I also wrote a song about family for a musical festival in Mexico. Last, but not least, there was a song that I wrote with my older sister just to convince my parents to give us a little more freedom during our teenage years. All of these songs used the same 4 chords! By the way, that last one didn't work very well.

In all honesty, even though I enjoyed the attention, lights, microphone and stage, I understood that this was not about me, but about the message of love and unity for a better world.

[Happy thought #5: Happiness has to do with looking beyond your-self.]

As kids we rarely stop to think: Who am I to do this or that? Am I good enough? What will people say? The negative thoughts and self-doubt that stop us as adults from pursuing our dreams and passions, fulfilling our mission and stepping up to our greatness rarely affect us when we are kids. The problem is, as we grow up, we start taking ourselves too seriously, and that's when we allow fear and perfectionism to prevent us from doing what deep down we know we ought to do.

What was your dream?
What were you passionate about?
Was there a special cause close to your heart?
Did you ever feel the calling to be a difference maker?

[Happy thought #6: Happiness is about stepping up to your great-ness.]

III. Avoid the Danger Zone

But years pass by and we grow up. We become adults and take on serious and important responsibilities, and we get busy. Money, work, bills, to-dos, we start building our "future". Some of us get lucky and marry our "Prince Charming". It is no longer about "my dreams" but "our dreams". Some of us embark on the adventure of parenthood which takes over most of our time and energy. It's all good and it's exciting. It is a little bit scary though, and confusing at times. Some of us experience an emotional roller coaster and feel thrilled and joyful one moment and cranky and overwhelmed the next.

We get busy. We get distracted. We forget about our main duty. The word "happiness" seems at times to be more of a luxury. It is something that we aspire to, but slips between our fingers. It is something important, but not urgent. We often think "I'll be happier when..." We start drifting towards the danger zone: survival mode.

[Happy thought #7: Success is not the key to Happiness; Happiness is the key to success.]

As I entered adulthood, I added more and more responsibilities to my list. In what felt like a blink of an eye, I was a wife, mom and an entrepreneur. They are three big words that put together meant A LOT of work!

Although I had the life I always wanted, I was stressed out and scared. Juggling all of these balls was a risky game, and I was horrified at the idea of dropping one and becoming "a failure". I didn't want to let down the people that I loved. Even with all the project management training I had, the aid of dozens of parenting sites and a few self-development programs, I still felt, at times, that my life was a mess and I had to get it under control.

[Happy thought #8: Happiness is not about achieving perfection, but deciding to look beyond imperfection.]

I was busy. Very busy. And tired. I was often grouchy, and had forgotten that the duty of happiness starts with myself, I had forgotten to smile more often. Strangely enough, it was in the face of adversity and trial that I started to find my way back to my purpose.

[Happy thought #9: Happiness is not the absence of difficulties, but a state of mind that allows you to feel positive in spite of them.]

IV. Stop seeking, start Creating.

Some people think they need to "seek", "find" or "pursue" happiness. The truth is that happiness is not misplaced, hiding or running away from us. It is not something we need to seek like we do with a missing sock or pursue like a train that gets away. Happiness is something we have the ability to create every single day of our lives. We all have the power to create happy moments for ourselves and moreover, to create the state of mind that allows us to feel joyful, grateful and at peaceful under any circumstances. We create happiness through our thoughts, actions and words. We can create it for ourselves and facilitate it for others.

[Happy thought #10: Happiness is an inside job.]

V. Write it with a capital L

Simply put, happiness is a synonym of LOVE, because LOVE is happiness' core nature. LOVE and happiness are inseparable. LOVE is happiness and happiness is LOVE. That is why we cannot acquire it with external aids. It comes from within. LOVE is the tool and the powerful weapon that we have within us to fulfill our happiness duty. LOVE is the answer to all the emptiness we can experience at any point in our life. The absence of LOVE is what makes us unhappy, and is most of the time manifested as fear, anger and despair. The greatest enemy of LOVE is fear... of loss, of not being good enough, of failure, etc.

Our level of happiness is directly proportional to the amount of LOVE in our life. There are numerous studies that we can refer to on the topic of happiness. Most of them show a correlation between happiness and the relationships that people have in their life, and very little with their external circumstances.

VI. Shape it like a Triangle

There are three main relationships we need to nurture in order to achieve true and sustainable happiness; the relationship with self, the relationship with our Creator and the relationship with others. This is what I call The Happiness Triangle™.

The Happiness Triangle™ shows the path to achieving true and sustainable happiness in good times and bad times; even in the face of difficulties. It is a perfect triangle with three equilateral sides; each corner represents the main sources of love, which are at the same time the main sources of happiness. They also represent the relationships we develop in a greater or lower proportion at different times in our life. These relationships hold the key to true and sustainable happiness:

Self-LOVE: Happiness starts within ourselves, knowing, understanding, accepting and loving ourselves, so we can get to know, understand, accept and love others and the world around us.

Supreme-LOVE: Happiness requires being humble enough to recognize that there is something greater than us.

Selfless-LOVE: True happiness cannot be achieved in isolation, but looking beyond ourselves and sharing other people's pain and joy.

VI. Embrace your "Happy-Mess"

At this point, I trust you know that I am talking about TRUE and SUSTAINABLE happiness. I am talking about the type that cannot be obtained through things or experiences. This is temporary and fades away easily, like the thrill and excitement of getting a new car, getting a promotion, or eating chocolate ice cream. I'm talking about fireproof happiness, the one that can withstand difficulties with peace and gratefulness, and fill your heart with joy when fulfilling your mission in life while loving and feeling loved.

Truth is, this type of happiness doesn't happen by chance. It takes focus and commitment. It also takes humility, embracing our imperfect human condition and a reliance on the Creator of the Universe and the people around us.

The term "Happy-Mess", reminds me that Happiness in this wounded world is only possible when I embrace my own mess and imperfection.

Only when I recognize that perfection is not a condition for happiness, can I be at peace with myself and others.

It is time to "pick a side" in the war against unhappiness. If you are in any way discontented with what's going on these days in our world and want to help create a happier one, you need to start with yourself. It is time to step into your greatness and start fulfilling your fundamental duty of happiness. Happy people can not only change their world; they can also change the world.

DECLARATION OF WAR AGAINST UNHAPPINESS

I hereby declare a war against unhappiness. I declare a war against indifference and victimhood. I declare a war against meaningless existence, survival mode, against not fulfilling the mission I've been created for.

I declare a war against hate, violence and against drugs that rot the soul of our youth; against useless role models and success stereotypes, I declare a war against the attempt of hatred to rule our world.

I declare a war against the fear of failure but mostly against the fear of success, against not stepping out to my greatness.

I declare a war against injustice, inequality, against kids not having water or shoes, but mostly against kids not being able to dream; against elder people feeling abandoned and lonely, against hollowness of soul, and not thinking beyond myself.

I declare a war against taking myself too seriously and not being silly from time to time; against losing my inner child.

I declare a war against not feeling responsible for our planet, destroying our ecosystem, and being hurtful to people and nature, against not being part of the solution.

I declare a war against war!

I declare a war against not taking responsibility over my own happiness... Starting TODAY.

MARIA GABRIELA JOVEL (GABY JOVEL) *is a Latina wife, mom and entrepreneur with a calling: to do her part in creating a happier world. She is a recorded artist and songwriter, former Miss El Salvador, and a professional with a degree in Marketing and Business Administration, and a Masters in Project Management obtained in Madrid, Spain.*

As part of her professional career, she worked for Microsoft Corporation for almost 10 years and got transferred to Miami to work in the Latin American headquarters. She left the company to become an entrepreneur and founded a successful Strategic Marketing & Project Management consulting firm (www. marketingpmo.com) to help companies accelerate their business growth and inspire her employees, contractors and clients to pursue life fulfillment. She is the author of "The Happiness Duty: Why happiness is NOT a Choice" (www. thehappinessduty.com).

Her life mission is to inspire women and their families to realize their inner power to pursue big dreams and to find true and sustainable happiness in order to create a better world. Her dream is to create a global movement to transform the world, one happy woman at a time.

Maria Gabriela Jovel (Gaby Jovel)
mgjovel@marketingpmo.com
www.marketingpmo.com
www.thehappinessduty.com

11

My Story

David Lerner, D.D.S.

When reflecting on our lives we can see a pattern emerge that reflects who we are. The events and challenges we have faced, what we chose to do in response...sometimes successful another times not.

Persistence is what matters, as Winston Churchill said...never give up, never ever give up.

I have been the one living my life but don't feel quite right taking the credit alone for all that I have become and achieved. None of us can take all the credit...if we grow and become successful, it will always be with support, encouragement, inspiration, and challenges presented by others. This has been the case for me. I grew up in a family impacted by chronic illness. My maternal grandfather Meyer was ravaged by the degeneration of Huntington's chorea which subsequently impacted my mother's sister and 3 of her 4 children. My father and his sister were both affected by multiple sclerosis, and then there was cancer which took the life of my grandfather, my father and my mother. My maternal grandmother Paula, who after her memory was destroyed by Alzheimer's disease, would greet me when I visited her in the nursing home with...I don't remember who you are but I love you anyway.

I felt lost as a kid and had trouble fitting in. I always felt that I marched to a different drummer. I was indifferent to school. I almost flunked out my first semester in college. I got motivated and found a sense of purpose. I wanted to understand more about life, the nature of it, how I came into creation and why I saw so much illness around me. I found something that for the first time in my life gave me a passion for understanding and learning. I became an A student after having been a C student most of my life.

I started college studying biology, learning about environmental sciences and geology, chemistry and cell biology If it had to do with the nature of life and the world within we live in, I wanted to know about it. Eventually my focus was drawn to the field then known as molecular biology. This had to do with the study of DNA, and all the events occurring on a molecular level within living things that allowed us to procreate, and to draw energy from our environment, our food etc. They were the mechanisms that sustained life in the most simple and at the same time the most complex way. I decided that I would be a mad scientist and became a research assistant to Professor Masayori Inoyue of the Department of Biochemistry at Stony Brook University. Though after a couple of semesters of work in the lab after classes, I began to feel that being a mad scientist was too isolating for me. I, therefore, decided to apply my interest and knowledge to the health sciences.

I didn't want to be a physician and to see so much chronic illness and death. I decided that I didn't want that. I chose dentistry instead.

My evolution as a holistic dentist began long before I had thought of becoming a dentist. It began when I was a kid. When I was going to the dentist, I would always have lots of cavities. It seemed like with every checkup there were more mercury silver fillings to be placed. Then, I needed braces. Because I had lost a tooth (a premolar) in my lower jaw due to an accident, the orthodontist decided to close the space by bringing my teeth all the way over in front from the right to the left. My teeth ended up looking straight but my jaw was crooked.

I had a difficult time in school. Everyone told me that I was an underachiever. Today, they might have recognized that I had a learning disability. I had difficulty processing information that I would read. It was a form of dyslexia— but more on that latter. I also had a difficult time with sports since I had poor coordination. I discovered years later that this all had a lot to do with the conditions in my mouth and how the rest of my body was being influenced by it.

Subsequent to my graduation with honors from dental school in 1978, I started to experience headaches and neck discomfort. It turned out to be related to the misalignment of my jaw. In the summer of 1980, I got a bite plate and some physical therapy. Everything seemed to be OK. My treating doctor was Dr. Richard Pertes, who now runs the Department of Craniofacial Pain at the New Jersey School of Dentistry and Medicine. Dick introduced me to Dr. Harold Gelb, who was a pioneer in the multi-disciplinary treatment of temporomandibular disorders. I was fortunate to work in Dr Gelb's office as an associate for 18 months.

It was during that time that my wife and I were living in Ossining. One winter there was a pretty good snow storm. Since we were newlyweds, we had not yet acquired all of the accouterments of a suburban household and did not have a snow shovel. Well, my car needed to be dug out of the snow. All I could find was a frying pan and so it went.

I injured my back, causing a subluxation between my lower lumbar spine and my sacrum. I was in pain. What made matters worse was that I could not find a practitioner who knew how to treat me. I saw chiropractors, physicians, and physical therapists. None of them could provide any relief. As time went on, the pain got worse and spread over more of my body. Eventually I had jaw and face pain, head pain, neck pain, and upper and lower back pain. I had pain shooting down my leg. It didn't matter if I stood, sat or laid down, the pain was unrelenting and wore me down.

Eventually I found Dr. Harold Briks. He was a chiropractor par excellence. He was an expert in the use of Applied Kinesiology and the Sacral-Occipital Technique. Applied Kinesiology is a biofeedback technique that uses the phenomenon of muscle reflex testing discovered by Dr. George Goodheart back in the 1960s. It allows a practitioner to diagnose disorders of the musculo-skeletal system with great efficiency and precision. The Sacral-Occipital Technique is a method of analysis of treatment of imbalances of the skull and sacrum developed by Dr. Major Dejarnette. These are discussed in more depth later on. From that very first visit with Dr. Briks, I started to experience relief. I was intrigued by his technique which he would use to get great results for me. I started to attend chiropractic seminars on Applied Kinesiology and to study how to apply it in my dental practice.

Although I was getting great relief from pain, I still wasn't feeling quite right and began to look elsewhere for additional answers. I experienced fatigue, and had poor digestion. I went to a dentist named Bob Poritsky who I knew practiced nutritional therapy. Bob was studying an interesting form of diagnosis based on the electrical conductance of acupuncture points. It was known as Electro-Acupuncture according to Voll. (eav). With this method, Bob was able to analyze the energetics of my body, gaining insight into the functional capacity of my organs, and to determine the likely causes of stress on my system. Bob told me that a major source of stress on my body was from mercury. I had heard of the potential for people to become ill from mercury from their fillings before. I subsequently had my mercury fillings removed and immediately felt some improvement energetically. As it turns out, this was the beginning of what became an odyssey of many years. I subsequently worked with health practitioners in many different fields, all along improving my health and developing an understanding of the role of interdisciplinary health care.

Over the years, I continued my study and training seeking to advance my skills in dentistry and to keep up with advances in dental technology. I also wanted to broaden and deepen my understanding of the inter-relationships between the mouth and the rest of the body. I have made it my mission to understand the relationship of the mouth and whole body health.

As I studied different approaches to healing from around the world, I recognized that there were common themes in all of them. They included: the need for healthful nourishment, the elimination of toxins, and the maintenance of physical, emotional, and energetic balance. These basic principles form the foundation for all holistic health practices.

Today, the field of biophysics has established that our bodies are quantum fields existing within the quantum field of the universe. In many cultures this has been known, and is expressed in ancient healing philosophies such as Ayurveda and Chinese Medicine. In these traditions of natural healing, the intent is to balance the flow of energy in the body and to develop higher levels of energetic integration throughout the system. This creates harmony between the individual and the world around them.

When disease is present, it may be viewed as evidence of a disruption in the life force. Rather than just treating the consequences of disease, a holistic practitioner is oriented to finding the cause and where possible, to assist the individual affected in reversing the disease process. The cause is often traced to an individual's lifestyle, diet, environment, attitudes and beliefs, etc. Once the causative factors are known and eliminated, the patient's natural healing forces will resolve the illness. Healing occurs from within the individual. It can not be imposed upon them.

Health is the consequence of the maintenance of an ordered state of our physiology over a period of time. Our organism is highly evolved to adapt to changes in various environmental conditions. The more extreme these conditions are, the more adaptation we need to make and the more our physiology is stressed. With sustained stress, our systems expend their adaptive capacities and the organization of the system decays. Health, therefore, is the ability of the system to maintain a highly organized state of function with the homeostatic capacity for preservation of that state.

Loss of health occurs as a result of a less than optimal state of function of the organism as a whole or as a result of deterioration of a component or components of the system's functional components. This results in a state of what we may call dysfunction.

Dysfunction of the organism or any of its components systems tends to lead to further loss of order. As a result, there is a serial decay of the integrity the organism as a whole. This process is what we commonly associate with the aging, although it is not truly aging. Human beings have the potential to maintain a highly functioning state of health throughout their life span, although this is a relatively uncommon experience.

The consequence of this deterioration of the functional integrity of the system; the loss of order and the deterioration of function ultimately leads to disruptions of the body energetically, biochemically, structurally, as well as on a cellular level. This ultimately creates the conditions we call chronic degenerative disease.

The science of biophysics has established that our bodies are quantum fields existing within the quantum field of the universe. In many cultures this has been known, and is expressed in ancient healing philosophies such as Ayurveda and Chinese Medicine. In these traditions of natural healing, the intent is to balance the flow of energy in the body and to develop higher levels of energetic integration throughout the system to create harmony between the individual and the world around them.

A holistically-trained dentist views the mouth as a micro-environment of the body with the profound potential to reflect and influence the health of the whole person. Disruptions to the flow of energy through the mouth may affect remote regions of the body, and conversely, disruptions elsewhere may manifest in the mouth. This occurs because the energy of our life force flows through all regions of the body permitting each to function as a hologram of the body as a whole. This forms the scientific basis for many healing disciplines such as Acupuncture, Kinesiology, Auricular Therapy, Iridology, Reflexology, etc. In Chinese medicine, analysis of changes within the tongue permit diagnosis of one's systemic condition. In the same way, regions of the mouth and individual teeth are found to correspond to particular meridians and organ systems.

As we evolve in our thinking and appreciation of the wholeness of our being, we begin to understand that what we view as the "mouth" is not limited to the teeth, gums, jaw, and associated temporomandibular joints and jaw muscles.

Structural imbalance or disharmony within the jaw and bite can have profound influences throughout the body as a whole. These imbalances can have profound influences within the musculo-skeletal system, the central nervous system, as well as through the body's electromagnetic energy circuits. As a consequence, proper treatment of TMJ and bite problems often requires a holistic team to support balancing the body as whole as the dentist works with the bite either through orthodontics (braces) or with crown and bridgework.

In the past few years, there has been a growing concern for the potential health hazards imposed by the use of dental materials that include toxic compounds. The most common source of concern has been the mercury found in silver fillings. Mercury is one of the most toxic metals found in nature and is a major component of silver fillings (up to 50%).

Organized dentistry has been reluctant to acknowledge the potential problems of toxic materials used in the mouth. The truth is that there are many variables. Each of us is different in the capacity of our body to eliminate toxins from our system. Because each of us presents a unique constitution, it is important that materials that are used in our mouths be screened to insure biocompatibility for us. Holistic dentists have a number of tools to use to do this. Sometimes blood tests may be used though they are not as precise as a simple biofeedback test done with Muscle Response Testing, or tests done with electro-dermal screening.

In the future, healthcare will not be care-focused on the treatment of advanced disease, but intent on the preservation of health. As Charles Mayo the founder of the world famous Mayo Clinic said in 1913;

> "It falls upon the dentist and oral surgeon to study the diseased conditions of the mouth. The work is discouraging, but must be kept up, as eventually it will have its effect. ...The next great step in medical progress in the line of preventive medicine should be made by the dentists. The question is will they do it?"

As we move forward dealing with the challenges of an aging population, with many in declining health, there is value in reflecting on the lessons to be learned from healing traditions from around the world. There are common principles to be applied. There is a clear health benefit to living our lives with an awareness and attunement to the natural world around us. It is health promoting to eat a diet of whole foods grown free of pesticides, antibiotics, and other contaminants. It is essential that our bodies stay free of toxins and pollutants, and maintain a healthy digestive and elimination system. It promotes good health to have proper posture and good habits in the exercise and rest of our bodies. Healthy self esteem promotes the choice of healthy habits and lifestyle.

I feel that I live a blessed life. I have learned from various mentors and many wonderful books I have read in ways that have enriched my awareness of the power of choice, of setting goals and living a life based on values and faith. I have felt empowered to listen to my inner voice and seeing the vision that I have been given. ▪

DAVID LERNER, DDS *graduated with honors from Temple University School of Dentistry in 1978. He has devoted his career to the practice of general dentistry with a focus on natural healing methods. In 2005, he founded the Center for Holistic Dentistry in Yorktown Heights, in New York's Westchester County. He and his wife Marisa reside nearby with their 3 cats. Their daughter, Donielle, is pursuing a career in the fashion industry.*

David L Lerner, DDS, C.Ac., F.I.N.D.
www.holisticdentist.com
914-245-4041

12

Who's The Boss?

Cheri Perry

Business Owner: it has a nice ring to it doesn't it? As a young business owner, the label carried a certain sense of authority, pride and even entitlement. You see, growing up in a successful family business had left its mark on me. I knew that if I was going to be 'anybody'—I had to strike out on my own and find a way to 'be the boss'. Little did I know that the self-employment journey I was about to embark on would be filled with all kinds of obstacles and experiences that would change my life and the lives of those around me.

THE BOSS:

Before I had any actual 'Boss like' experience, I had already made several assumptions about what being a business owner would be like. Obviously, I would have complete control of my time. It would give me the flexibility that we all long for. Even just typing that last sentence makes me laugh out loud! I know that as a business owner you do get to work half days and you can either pick the first 12 or the second 12! After the initial start up, I would have plenty of cash to do whatever I wanted to do. I was not prepared to change what I 'wanted' to do so drastically! Finally, I envisioned all of my plans materializing with effort (of course) but I did not see any big challenges on the horizon. After all, I grew up with a serial entrepreneur and it was a sure bet that this kid was paying attention! In fact, the 'sipping margaritas poolside' scenario often seen on television, seemed like just a few bright business decisions away! Now for the rest of the story!

Our first business was a cleaning company with which we had early success. (Incidentally, the other part of WE is my husband, my better half Dean—how the marriage survived this first grand adventure is another story!). We landed a large commercial client and were faced with the enviable position of having more work than we could handle. So we became employers. Just the thought of how my younger self dealt with this new title, makes me squirm a bit in my seat! In those early years, I definitely felt that THE BOSS's job was to dictate orders and the staff's job was to follow my carefully thought-out edicts. I was an expert at spouting off orders and sounding as if I were in charge. It seemed simple—I tell you what to do and you simply do what you are told. It's no wonder that the biggest issue we had in our business revolved around staffing—or was it my leadership style. Hmmmm? Today I know the answer but years ago I was convinced that all good workers resided in states other than my own and I had the ex-employee list to prove it. It's funny how time reveals the true reasons behind both success and failure in business. It took many years, but eventually the 'problems' I blamed on staffing (as well as a myriad of other situations), soon revealed HERSELF in the mirror. But before she could be dealt with, there were a few smaller issues to contend with.

THE GOVERNMENT:

While Dean and I had both heard about the government, we knew very little about them and even less about what we were supposed to pay them. So when we received notice that we owed one MILLION dollars in back taxes (OK, so it wasn't that much but it sure seemed like it at the time), I scheduled an appointment with the appropriate tax mongers and was stunned when they did not see the logic in my argument. 'You show me what work you did to EARN that money and I will figure out a way to pay it.' They couldn't prove 5 minutes of work let alone earning the money they wanted and so I did what all novice business owners do- I threw a temper tantrum and paid the bill over time. It only took one tax levy to figure out that taxation was ALWAYS going to be a part of the puzzle—not a problem per se—but definitely a budgeting item.

PREMATURE CELEBRATION:

Once we had the tax issue resolved and a method in place for replacing underperforming (or staffers who could not tolerate strong'leadership') team members, we did what any successfully stupid business owner would do—we bought a boat! Yes, in the two years that we had slaved away, we managed to learn the art of delegation and over-spending. It is important to note (since my husband may read this) that over-spending is his term and definition for something I like to refer to as a depositing problem. At least in the early part of my learning curve, I felt that any money issues simply meant we were not making enough! I should ask Dean to write an entire book on finances and the fiscally flawed! But enough about me… After assigning the workload to our revolving group of staff members, we began spending many of our days with our new boat. In our book, we had 'Arrived'. I think it is important to mention that we had plenty of all night work days because the staffers failed to do their job and so WHAT GOES UP…you know the rest!

We had arrived all right but we had no idea where. In a relatively short period of time, the industry shifted and the large commercial contract we built our business around began to diminish. We had no processes, no real procedures, no sound accounting practices and we ended up almost sleeping in that boat!! At this time, we had all the business acumen that a starving first time business owner would have (very little) and so we did the most logical thing: we ended up deciding to do something different—something that did not require those pesky employees— and we started business number 2.

ONE IS THE LONELIEST NUMBER

In our new adventure, we decided that we would do the work ourselves (there's a brilliant long-term strategy for you!). We sold cellular phones and just like the first business, we were successful almost right out of the gate. Dean and I were very good at sales and we ALWAYS delivered a great service so we started with our old cleaning clients and got a good running start. We worked long days and were able to make some forward progress fiscally but we always seemed to be on the edge financially and our marriage was taking some strong hits. I guess Dean did not appreciate the strong leadership I carried over from the last business. We were both feeling the pressure of marital strain, so we did what any business couple would do—we added another business.

SUCCESSFUL AND SEPARATING:

For the next several years, we dabbled in both businesses until we decided to focus in one direction and our third business was born the same year that our son Tyler was—a VERY busy year on many levels. Thinking that the two businesses were to blame for the stress in our marriage, we elected to shut the phone business down and reduce a little stress but it did not help. By the time Tyler was 2, our marriage was FLAT, our business was stagnating and we were both thinking about the D word. That's when I took the trip to Dallas that altered our world forever. (That story can be found in Ziglar First Class). I will give you this nugget however-God is still in the miracle business!

TRUE LEADERSHIP:

Over time, I realized that barking orders to people and expecting them to just know what I expected didn't work. I am sad to say that many amazing people have come and gone due in large part to my poor interpretation of what leadership is and what being the boss really means. I don't even want to think of the damage I might have caused by the way I spoke to people in those early years. Even now, heartfelt tears are falling from my eyes as I realize the opportunities I missed to add value instead of drama. To fill up instead of squeeze out. The greatest joy of my life today (aside from my rockin' hubby and that beautiful man child I handcrafted) is finding ways to contribute to the lives of those I've been entrusted with (thank you Bob Beaudine for asking the question "What are you doing with the people God gave you?). For too many years. I used the people up and spit them out—nicely, of course, but the end result was the same; those were missed opportunities to develop and cherish people. Today, life is different for us, for our team and for anyone who will stand still long enough for me to add a little value. My mentor Zig Ziglar was right—you truly can have everything in life you want, if you just help enough other people get what they want and guess what? We ALL want to feel needed!

THE BOSS?

Yes, we decided that we could not do everything ourselves and became employers again. While great leadership is about constantly improving and sharpening your skills, I've come to realize that, in those early days, I was the problem. It would have been magnificent to have had Disney's Magic mirror so my leadership journey might have been shortened! I can imagine being called to task by that truth telling reflection...

> Mirror Mirror on the wall
> Who's the best leader of them all?
> Not me you say but I'm the boss!
> I say when, I bare the cost
> of every staff mistake and blunder
> I keep us afloat or we go under
> Leadership is not position, or telling others what to do.
> The very best leader will be found HERE
> when you learn to work on you!

Ouch and oh so true! The change did not happen in the blink of an eye and I will forever be a work in progress. However, when I got clear on the fact that the universe did not revolve around me and that being the BOSS was more of a responsibility than I had ever dreamed, our world started changing rapidly. We began to attract strong dreamers who opened themselves up for feedback. We had a lot less friction and way more fun, Today we have a phenomenal team of dedicated professionals. We have processes and procedures in place to systematize our business so we really CAN leave without taking away from our bottom line and we do what my friend Howard Partridge has helped us to do: empower our team, create leaders and have a LIFE (Living In Freedom Every day) outside of our business.

THE GOVERNMENT:

I would love to tell you that my many temper tantrums yielded a nice reduction in our tax bill but that would just be a daydream. Over the years, we DID learn to plan for our taxes and yours truly did something I should probably have done much sooner. I left the money management in the hands of a gifted, albeit frugal, guy named Dean Perry! He has a knack for that portion of the business and rather than being the control freak that I was for a lot of years, I stepped aside and let the true leader in that area, lead. Funny how the government leaves you alone and how your business (and marriage) prospers when you get out of your own way.

WHAT GOES UP- WITH CARE CONTINUES!
ONE IS NOW A GREAT NUMBER

Remember how I said we got a second business and then eventually decided to focus on ONE?

My parents bought us an amazing piece of art that listed a Chinese proverb just below the wings of an American Bald Eagle. It says "If you chase two rabbits both will escape. "Well this was actually a good call way back then. Combining our efforts, streamlining our processes and getting on the same page radically changed the landscape of our lives and the lives of our team. Drama in the workplace is not only a buzz killer but it is also a productivity killer especially when that drama starts at the top!

SUCCESSFUL - FOR REAL

Early on, our definition of success revolved around things like having a boat, being the boss and how much money we made. MAN, have things changed! Today success is something that we cherish and the definition has changed. Living our lives so that they make a difference in the lives of those we serve, those who serve us and those we just happen upon; that sounds like REAL success—achieving your goals and dreams by participating in the lives of others and making a real difference.

DIFFERENCE MAKERS:

Being a business owner does have a nice ring to it and I highly recommend the journey as long as you are ready to roll up your sleeves and start with the man or woman in the mirror!

Today, we view employment as a two-way street and we work our hearts out to provide an amazing opportunity for those who choose our company as their work home.

Today, we view crafting a business as a mission to see how many lives we can impact in a positive manner.

Today we take a much more structured approach to growing our business, so opportunities exist for others. We feel very blessed to participate in the personal and professional success of our team.

Today, we take care of each other and truly love the constant and never-ending growth (thank you for that insight Anthony Robbins) that is present in our lives.

Today, we have replaced entitlement with a serious desire to empower the lives of everyone we touch. We hope that this sliver of our story has created hope in yours. And that pool side beverage? Haven't given it a thought in years but I can imagine the kids of our team all splashing around that pool with their happy parents… Now, that's what I call a boss's happy ending!

We were all placed on this planet to touch the lives of our fellow humans and we can only achieve that goal when we step up and in to our greatness. God bless and thank you for spending a few minutes with me today!! I would love to hear about your story! I'll bet you are a Difference Maker too! ▨

CHERI PERRY *lives in Battle Ground, Wash., with Dean Perry, her husband of 25 years. Their son, Tyler Perry, is pursuing a career in aviation and is a student at Montana State University. Cheri grew up in a family business and has owned several businesses with her husband. Their current business, Total Merchant Concepts is a national credit-card processing company that provides a variety of business services to merchants and credit unions and celebrated its 20th year in 2016. The success of the Perry family business and Cheri's love of public speaking have provided many opportunities for her to present on topics ranging from "Small Business Success" to "Passionate Partnerships." Her personal passion for excellence in service, business development, heartfelt leadership, and relationships is something she lives and loves to share. Cheri is a Certified Ziglar Legacy Trainer, A John Maxwell Certified Trainer, a Certified Behavioral Consultant with Jim Rohn and a Distinguished Toastmaster.*

CHERI PERRY
Cheri@CheriPerry.com
www.CheriPerry.com
360-980-0392

13

GETFITGETRICH™
A Story about a Fitness and Finance Movement Designed to Inspire and Empower Others

Claudia Saillant and Maria M. Lopez

THE ALARMING SITUATION

Did you know that the United States has one of the highest rates of child obesity in the world? Did you know that a large percentage of the U.S. Hispanic community is overweight? Did you also know that the large majority of U.S. Hispanics are not saving enough for their retirement years?

We live in a world where we no longer have time to prepare our own healthy meals, where most of the foods are processed and packaged in a can or a box, and where there is a fast food restaurant at every corner in America. Many organizations are not making us aware of the importance of the health issues that are associated with these trends. In addition, we are not exercising enough and the majority of our children are playing outside less and less.

Another issue is the financial situation of many U.S. Hispanics who are most likely living paycheck to paycheck, and are not saving enough for retirement. Many young Hispanics graduating from colleges and universities in recent years have accumulated a large amount of student debt and are not finding the jobs to support themselves. When it comes to retirement savings, Latinos are failing. That's what many recent surveys by financial institutions and other organizations reveal. In many ways, these surveys echo what has been laid out in many previous minority retirement studies. While all populations find retirement planning to be an overwhelming task, Hispanics feel the least prepared. Approximately 54 percent of all Hispanics feel they are "not very" or "not at all" prepared. A total of 18 percent of them say they're still on the sidelines and have not started saving for retirement.

THE MISSION IS CREATED

These alarming statistics and trends are what inspired Claudia Saillant and Maria M. Lopez to create the movement, GETFITGETRICH™. The movement, born in South Florida, is designed to create awareness and to educate the U.S. Hispanic community by empowering them to create the lives of their dreams.

Claudia, born and raised in the Dominican Republic, and Maria M. Lopez, born in Nicaragua and raised in South Florida, both live in Miami, FL. They have discovered their individual passions and life's purpose. Claudia Saillant and Maria M. Lopez met in the summer of 2015 while attending a South Florida event for those who aspire to become public speakers. Claudia's individual mission is to empower divorced women to rebuild their own personal lives while building the body of their dreams. Maria's individual mission is to empower the U.S. Hispanic community by providing them with financial education and services. They are now mentoring each other, are combining their strengths and they dare to make a difference in a joint mission.

CLAUDIA'S STORY

Claudia, founder of Get Your Divorced Body, is a speaker, professional power lifter and fitness coach and mentor. Her passion is to empower divorced women to re-build their own personal lives while building the body of their dreams. She meets with her clients at a boutique gym in

Pinecrest, South Florida, where she trains them several times a week. She also offers them guidelines in nutrition, and leads them through motivational and educational weekly conference calls. Her program, which can range from three months to one year, is available to both women and men. Claudia's program also offers vision boarding, pantry fridge makeovers, fitness and grocery shopping sprees and much more.

Get Your Divorce Body is a fitness movement, designed to inspire women who are going through divorce or have been divorced who want to transform their bodies and create a new life. As a public speaker, Claudia is motivating and inspiring women through her sharing of her own life story and by providing them with her fitness tips and recommendations.

Joy, fitness and a passion to help others describe Claudia's personality and strength. She believes in making a difference in the lives of women by inspiring them with her life's story of overcoming difficult times and re-building herself. Claudia, who was divorced after a 10-year marriage, had not previously designed nor monitored her finances until one day she became a single mom. Despite friends and families and other medical professionals offering medication, Claudia stayed strong in using balanced nutrition and fitness to pull herself from the painful life experience that divorce generally brings.

Claudia is currently growing her business in Miami, while also pursuing her career as an inspirational public speaker. She has also has been interviewed for articles in local newspapers and magazines.

Claudia's clients include women of all ages and backgrounds. One of her clients came to her because she wanted to look beautiful on the most important day of her life: her wedding. This particular client was very skinny and she wanted to sculpt her body so she could feel fit and look fabulous in her wedding gown. In just four months, she gained 10 pounds for her wedding day on February 13, 2016. Other clients of Claudia are looking for ways to lose weight, build muscle and maintain their new fitness and nutrition habits.

MARIA'S STORY

Maria, founder of the Life-style Finances for Entrepreneurs, has been a tax consultant for 20 years working in public accounting delivering accounting and income tax solutions to multi-national organizations. Maria discovered her purpose aligned with her passion, which is to provide financial education and services to the U.S. Hispanic community so that they can build the lives of their dreams. Maria launched her own accounting firm, Gallant Accountants and Advisors located in Miami, FL that provides a variety of financial services and solutions to Hispanic women entrepreneurs. Maria also provides financial planning education to the community through her website, social media, webinars, and in live presentations on various stages.

Maria's passion to help and empower others is centered on utilizing her work experiences, talents and a strong desire to make a difference in the lives of those who lack financial education and training.

Maria advises her clients, entrepreneurs and business owners, on their accounting, finances, and financial growth strategies. Maria works with her clients, who reside anywhere in the United States, skypes with her clients and meets with them on a regular basis. As a good listener, Maria is in-tune with her clients' financial and emotional situations, and promotes suggestions and recommendations for her clients to choose from so that together they can create the desired outcomes and financial situations. Maria's entrepreneur clients come to her seeking direction, organization, clarity, knowledge and awareness, and they are able to walk away with all of that plus with financial security, and the possibility of living in financial independence.

COLLABORATION BEGINS

"I realized that as I made a decision to communicate and share my message of financial education, from a platform or a stage, I had to conquer the fear of public speaking and become physically fit again so that those in the audience and in my community would be inspired to take action in creating the lives of their dreams" Maria said to Claudia. "I want to work with you as my fitness coach so that I can build a fit and healthy body."

Empowered to make a difference in Maria's life, Claudia began coaching Maria in the gym doing strength training and cardio. They both knew this would be a journey but they were not aware of the miracle of friendship and how being around energy rich, like-minded people could create and build a movement that would empower others, as they were empowering themselves. One day they recorded their first #Get Fit Get Rich Facebook video while hanging out in the gym's locker room.

Their weekly motivational videos are aimed at inspiring their Facebook friends and social media followers by providing tips and best practices in fitness and in finances. Their goal and purpose is to create a movement larger than their two individual brands that will result in their clients and Facebook friends and followers building a strong, sexy and healthy body and the lifestyle finances of their dreams.

The lesson that Maria and Claudia are learning is in the strength and benefit that exists when someone inspires and supports another person in a developing area of their lives. They are leading, guiding each other, and supporting each other in their own journey of transformation in the areas of fitness and finances.

They are bringing their talents, experiences and passion to their communities through education and coaching. They realized that they needed to request support in the areas where they were weak and then they are also utilizing their own strengths to contribute to the lives of others.

WHY WE ARE DOING THIS

"Our goal is to promote awareness and self-confidence in the areas of fitness and finances. We realize that we do not have a long-standing history of being public speakers. However, we have a great message to share and are driven by our own life experiences and the passion to make a difference," said Claudia and Maria.

Our goal is to empower members of the U.S. Hispanic community to address issues in their finances and fitness, to take control of them, to own them and to create a new desired lifestyle from this awareness and education. With our GETFITGETRICH™ movement, we would like to extend it to the entire U.S. population and beyond (the planet).

Making a difference in someone else's lives is something many are doing every day. This could include: providing a smile to a stranger, offering your seat to another person, coaching your children's school soccer team, saying "I love you", hiring for employment someone who has no permanent home, or creating a movement bigger than ourselves that leaves a legacy in humanity and changes the course in people's lives for the better. Making a difference begins with believing in ourselves. It begins with having an awareness of what we believe to be right and wrong.

"We believe we have a choice! In every moment of our lives, we choose how we live in how we behave, in what we say, and in what we do", said Claudia and Maria.

Maria and Claudia have a choice. They can either continue to live their lives ignoring their passion and purpose, or they can choose to take action, be driven, fearless, reach for something bigger than themselves and to be somewhere they had never been before.

Both Maria and Claudia realize they are responsible for the outcomes of their choices. Today, while Claudia coaches and mentors Maria in her exercise routine and building new eating habits, Maria guides and leads Claudia in designing her finances through creating a financial plan for her life's goals and in replacing bad habits with good financial habits.

OUR CALL TO ACTION

With only a few months since their first GETFITGETRICH™ video was launched, there are many results of their movement. It includes clients, friends and family members who are sharing their comments on being inspired to take action in joining a gym and start exercising, cooking their own healthy meals, writing their own financial budgets, and asking Claudia and Maria questions for their advice, recommendations and best practices in the areas of finance and fitness. Claudia's clients are adopting new healthy eating habits and building a strong and fit body by exercising periodically. Maria, one of Claudia's clients, has also lost approximately 15 pounds. Maria's clients are receiving support, assistance and services in the areas of finance and now have access to someone who makes available to them information and data about their businesses so they can make wiser and better informed decisions.

Both Maria and Claudia believe in the strength of being surrounded and empowered by like-minded people. They also believe in the power of creating alliances and relationships that will allow them to achieve their life's purpose and goals. But most of all, they believe in the miracle of friendship. If you would like to reach out to Claudia and Maria and or join their movement, you can find them on their Facebook page at #GETFITGETRICH™. Their GETFITGETRICH™ quarterly events are held for entrepreneurial women and men who are seeking to get fit and get rich.

Our call to action is to get you inspired to take action in your lives and other peoples' lives by contributing your strengths to assist and lead others. This is about giving! It's about Paying it Forward! It's about service! Serving our community, our children and the generations to come!

It's about elevating the U.S. Hispanic community and creating opportunities in their lives. It's about spreading a message of initiative and action. ■

CLAUDIA SAILLANT,

(right) founder of Get Your Divorce Body ("GYDB"), is a body-sculpting expert, power-lifting gold medalist and empowered divorcee mother of two. Get Your Divorce Body is a uniquely designed program that reveals the secrets of the pros and models a lifestyle beyond the conformity of traditional diet and exercise techniques.

GYDB is a fitness movement designed to inspire divorced women to create a new life for themselves so that divorce becomes the best thing that could ever have happened to them.

Claudia's story:

Five years into a decade-long marriage and fully thrusted into motherhood, Claudia awoke to find herself overweight, deeply unhappy and completely lost. She began down a path of finding herself again through diet and exercise. Her transformation resulted in Claudia looking absolutely amazing and strong and also feeling whole and empowered in her life and all relationships.

Through her own transformation and empowerment, Claudia has remained strong through the most devastating phase of her life: a difficult divorce after 10 years of marriage, which produced 2 beautiful children. She has come out of her divorce gracefully by discovering her own passion supporting women to transform their physical strength into emotional strength.

Through her unique Get Your Divorce Body program, Claudia coaches divorced women to shift their mindset, resulting in amazing forgiveness, happiness and empowerment.

Claudia shows women how to create a new life by design that benefits their families, relationships and gives them the tools to be beacons of strength for others. Oh, and they also look super-hot.

MARIA M. LOPEZ, *(left) is changing the way that Hispanics think about finance.*

As founder of Lifestyle Finances for Entrepreneurs and owner of Gallant Accountants and Advisors, Maria teaches Hispanic entrepreneurs how to design a lifestyle through their finances. Her clients build their finances, grow their businesses and empower the Hispanic community through their financial leadership.

Maria, born in Nicaragua, discovered her life's purpose, through a combination of her passion to give back to the Hispanic community through financial tools and education and her experience, which included 22 years in public accounting.

Maria's signature system breaks down the complexity of finance and focuses on building a legacy and future for her clients' vision.

Maria's perseverance and dedication started at age 6 when she would see her mother coming back from the office after a long day at work. She remembers seeing her mother in a beautiful dress, high heels and a brief case. Maria knew then that her future life as an adult was to be a successful entrepreneur.

On top of an extensive career in public accounting, Maria holds a certificate as a Florida Certified Public Accountant, a Masters degree in Taxation and a Bachelors of Science degree in Accounting from Florida International University. She is a candidate for the Certified Financial Planner certification and considers herself a lifelong student. She is passionate about empowering the Hispanic community financially and building wealth for Hispanic entrepreneurs and families.

Maria lives in Miami, Florida where she speaks on issues of finance for the Hispanic community.

Claudia Salliant
cmariesaillant12@gmail.com
305-778-5778

Maria M. Lopez
maria.lopez@cpa.com
305-321-6578

14

Make a U-Turn!
Ashley Truitt

"Make a U-Turn" - I Dare You!

We all know that "Life is about the Journey and not the Destination," right? I also believe that there are many paths within the journey that guide and challenge us to hopefully achieve where we want to be in life. I have been presented with a number of what I describe *"Forks in the Road"* while marching through my journey. I have experienced firsthand the realization and importance of continuing to evaluate the path you are on and even more critically, if it is not working for you *"Make a U-Turn!"*. It's OK to recalibrate and change your path. Invest in yourself, dig deep and be honest. *"Mistakes are a wise person's education!"*

I Knew I had to Recalibrate When...

...my husband said to me, "This is ridiculous, you are always at work, this job was meant to give you more time at home and it is now worse than when you were on the road. You need to resign and you need to do it tomorrow," came as quite a shock to say the least. I looked at him surprised while thinking to myself, is this a good thing or am I offended? For some women, that statement would be music to their ears. However, I wasn't hearing any Symphonies! My instant defense and response was something to the tune of "well that's easy for you to say, this is my career you are talking about." My twenty-five-year career flashed before my eyes with a brightness resembling a Target Red Light Special highlighting and exposing all of my insecurities. I thought to myself... *"really, have all my efforts led to such insignificance?"*

The Early Years

Born in Singapore to a British father and South African mother, my family was living in Singapore while my father completed a contract with a globally-renowned advertising agency as the Managing Director for South East Asia. Not really recollecting my own memories as a baby of our fabulous life there, family photographs were plentiful during my childhood and I learned through later conversations of the fond memories my parents had of their time spent there. My brother Jason was five and I was three, when we moved back to Johannesburg, South Africa. Back then it was still a safe place to live. We lived in a lovely big home on an acre of land with an in-ground trampoline and a lovely big pool which also posed nicely as a prime setting and location for many an extravagant "Ad Agency" party. However, after some years, the advertising life was starting to take a toll on my parents. As a result, they made the decision that it was time for a change and that we would move to the beautiful Cape to be by the sea.

Magnificent Cape Town undoubtedly has some of the world's most spectacular beaches and great places to live, certainly in the 1970's. We lived right on the ocean in a place called St. James, where I went to school at Star of the Sea Convent. Yes, I had real nuns who wore habits, always had a ruler in their hand and were surprisingly fierce! Both Jason and I were doing well at school, enjoying life growing up at the beach with lots of friends and plenty of extra curricular activities.

After living in the Cape for a few years, my Dad took a new senior executive position with a company that would in later years offer a big opportunity and a relocation for our family to Sydney, Australia.

Sydney was breathtaking. Driving over the Harbour Bridge and looking down at the stunning Opera House was a memorable experience and I still clearly remember the feeling to this day. We were all excited to be in Sydney but it wasn't long before our comfortable new family life began to see problems on the horizon. My parents started fighting, Dad would stay longer and later at the office, Jason seemed to be getting into trouble frequently and I was charging full steam ahead into the "terrible teen" years! Although there were some very happy "normal" times as a family, it would be another two years of growing family discord.

Throughout my high school years, I would always ask my Dad if I could go and work at his office. This became a regular occurrence over the school holidays, doing a variety of jobs, mostly administrative type work. I thoroughly enjoyed the people, the comradery and the overall work environment.

Leading up to the end of my last year of high school (year ten), I had the option of transferring to a private girls school or go to a business college. Starting with secretarial college which after a while I found highly boring, I ultimately found a job as a dental nurse and enrolled to get my Certificate in Dental Nursing while training on the job and attending school two nights a week at a local dental school for a couple of years. This was the beginning of what became a long-standing career.

Tragedy Strikes

It was in my first year working as a dental nurse, when our family was turned upside down at the sudden death of my beautiful, talented, quick- witted and fiercely intelligent Mum (Molly). She had committed suicide on my seventeenth birthday. Although I sincerely believe that my birthday didn't hold any significance, it was just that day where in her mind she could no longer be. Jason was interstate at the time in Queensland and I will never forget the phone call I had to make from the neighbor's house telling him that Mum was gone and he needed to come home quickly. Like most of us at seventeen, we are just not equipped nor prepared for how to deal with such tragic loss. I had no idea which direction to turn or how to deal with feelings of sheer emptiness, guilt and loss! We were all devastated. Both Mum and Dad were only children so we didn't have any aunts, uncles or any other family in the country. However, we have some wonderful long standing family friends who were there in an instant to help with the days that lay ahead of us. Jason arrived later that evening. My heart ached for him at the fact he was on his own and had to fly back home knowing what was awaiting him and dealing with the loss of his Mum. That night, our friends insisted that we all come to stay with them. I recall very vividly sitting around the dinner table, reminiscing and telling stories about my Mum. We laughed, we cried and it actually felt quite cathartic for us all. At one point, the eldest son of that family, aged nineteen, stood up and said quite upset"you know I have to say I'm mad at Molly, she left us without saying goodbye…"

"Suicide is such a lonely and desperate measure to those who feel or believe they have no other way out, there are always options in life and no one should have get to a point and carry a burden of such helplessness."

That year we all went our separate ways not knowing what to do or how to console each other of our grieving needs, so we just didn't really talk about it. Although still living in our family home, we had limited family unity and schedule together.

To that day, I have very happy and secure memories as a child with loving parents who were actively involved in everything we did. It was a life that was filled with opportunity and for that I will always be grateful.

And so I now began my journey in a new life that I never expected…

My reaction was survival, strength and independence. I knew that if I needed any form of help, my Dad was always there for me no matter what. However, I was now seventeen years old, a grown up, working and carving out my own life making decisions, some good and admittedly some bad!

Around that time, I had an opportunity to take a job in Melbourne which was several hours from Sydney, and of course, my Dad. I remember feeling guilty and sad leaving my Dad and our family home.

However, he was occupied and moving on with his life too, so I continued on with the plan.

My new job in Melbourne was in the dental/orthodontic manufacturing business. I was excited to start and really engage in something with stability and the opportunity of growth, promotion and overall to be successful. *"A great distraction to a heavy heart!"*

I threw myself into work, learned a lot, worked very hard, got promoted and was hungry for more. After four years' experience with this company and just twenty-one years old, my boss asked me if I would like to go to Singapore to set up a business replicating the one we had in Melbourne. I immediately thought it was a positive sign to go back to my birthplace and hopefully connect with something in finding peace with my Mum. I was a little anxious yet very much looking forward to having such responsibility being entrusted to me. I agreed to the contract and off I went to Singapore. A year passed quickly, with the business operational and making money. A local general manager was employed to take over the operations which would then allow me to move on to the next venture. With an airline ticket back to Australia, I decided to take a week off and stopped in lovely Bali, Indonesia to do some thinking and clear my head for what I really wanted to pursue next. However, before I could even get home to Australia, I had a job offer to go to the UK. As a result, I didn't invest any time thinking about where I really was and what I wanted for my future. What are my hopes and dreams and how do I fulfill them?

Because my focus was on work, which really trumped everything in my path, I didn't give much thought to the job itself, other than that I was excited. I hadn't been to London since I was a child, had a British Passport and again I thought it was another positive sign for me personally. I, therefore, made the decision quickly to accept the offer. Two weeks later, on an eighteen-hour flight to London, I thought to myself half way across the world "really, what are you doing?"

I know what I was doing. I was running away so that I wouldn't have to deal with grieving and the deepened sadness of losing my Mum. My career was becoming a mask for my identity, that was my focus and my defense mechanism. I had lost a part of "Me" and I didn't nurture who I really was or who I wanted to be.

I spent seven years in the UK which was a tremendous experience personally and for my career. There were many wonderful places that I visited in Europe and met many great friends who are still a very special part of my life today. I always knew that I would one day leave the UK and head back to Australia, which I did.

More Tragedy

During this time, my dear brother Jason had been battling a heroin addiction for some years and had contracted AIDS from non-sterile needles. He took an overdose one day which was yet another utterly devastating blow for my Dad, myself and his girlfriend. However, he pulled through, although highly compromised, and lived for two more years in a hospital. We are not sure whether the overdose was to end it all or not. His girlfriend didn't think it was intentional since they had recently made some plans that they were both excited about for the future, including him being sober. He passed away the first year that I was in the UK. I remember getting the call from my Dad and feeling that my heart couldn't have ached or hurt anymore. I miss him so terribly. He was my big brother who looked after me. I miss his wicked sense of humor and the phone calls from Rehab asking me to listen to him playing the guitar or piano. I miss his loving nature, free spirit and just for being an extraordinary person in his short twenty-seven years. *I always will wonder if we didn't take the fork in the road that led to Australia, would Mum and Jason still be alive?*

It felt great arriving back on Australian soil, even though it wasn't Sydney. I had accepted a job in Melbourne prior to my leaving the UK. After a year in Melbourne, desperately wanting to get back to Sydney, I set up a satellite office and finally felt as though I was going home after twelve years. Ready to stake some roots in the soil!

This was a new beginning for me. I was now thirty years of age and ready to settle down. Through my connections working internationally, I was introduced to a young man named John. Also in the dental industry and independently successful, John was living in Texas and traveled to the UK regularly for business. He called me out of the blue one day, said that he had just moved to Sydney and was setting up a business similar to the companies I had worked for before. He asked me if I would like to join his team with a good offer and a stake in the company. It was too good an opportunity to pass up! This savvy, witty and extremely smart young man would soon became the love of my life and we were married on Manly Beach, Sydney, Australia in 2003.

The next thirteen years would be a whirlwind of career highs and lows. One of the highs for both John and I, was accepting the role of founding executives in the creation and listing of a medical device company on the Australian Stock Exchange in 2004. Who would have thought that my roots as a dental nurse would eventually lead to this? It was an amazing career experience, much like getting your MBA in real time! There were times of great satisfaction and feeling like it was a job well done, to times of uncertainty where insecurities would creep in and I would doubt myself. At times it just wasn't comfortable, nor did it come naturally…*But I did it, you dig deep find the strength, confidence and muster through it!*

In 2006, we relocated to Texas to build the Australian company and launch it in the US market, with John as CEO and myself as the VP of Business Development. As the years went by, I started to feel stuck in what I was doing. It became more of a necessity to now earn a big salary which was motivated by an indulgent lifestyle that we had created to balance the crazy twenty-four-seven corporate grid we were living in, secretly in misery! These were hard times emotionally where I felt as though I was nearing the end of this particular road and knew that I had to make some changes to find an alternative route. *Again I did what my defense mechanism told me, keep trying harder and harder, strive for something bigger…."*

I Decided to Make a U-Turn

Ten years later and back to my opening Chapter... I agreed with John to resign from my job and my career. I was finally able to take a step back, take a deep breath, think and understand what is important to me, my marriage, my family, my friends and life in general. I feel so fortunate and will be forever grateful to John for pushing me.

Quite serendipitously and just earlier this year, a dear friend Michelle Prince invited me to attend her "BookBound by the Sea" program in Captiva Island FL, held once a year in January and always a huge sell out. The seminar teaches you how to get a book out of your head and onto paper, how to become a top-selling author and the expert in your field! Fantastic, I was motivated and excited to attend the class. However, I will admit that in the pit of my stomach, I had this burning fear of *"what is my field or industry now, what am I going to write about, I left my career... **I have no identity!"***

After digging deep and being totally inspired from the "BookBound" weekend, I put on my big-girl pants, grabbed my brave stick, started to think and write about my journey, the paths I chose and the sadness I ran from. Recognizing the reality of chasing something that I thought would bring happiness and security in having a successful, busy career hit me right between the eyes.... *My hopes and dreams had been buried in an emotional block and I never allowed myself the time to recognize them, or nurture them until now.*

At this pivotal moment, and after many discussions, I realized that I wasn't alone. There are so many other people who think they are stuck on a path that doesn't feel right...a path that ultimately won't lead them where they want to go. History will repeat itself until we learn from it, so I encourage you to make a "U-Turn" and recalibrate your route. *It's never too late to change your direction!*

Now 48 years old, I feel *free*, totally empowered and looking forward to helping others find and nurture their hopes and dreams too.

I stepped outside of my comfort zone and "Dared to be a Difference Maker"...now, I double dare you! ◾

ASHLEY TRUITT, *from Sydney Australia, has over 25 years in the dental industry where she has held directorships and executive management positions in both private and publicly held companies. Ashley has extensive international business experience with an accomplished track record in Startup and Business Development, Operations and Management.*

With a degree in Marketing and Business, Ashley was instrumental in the creation and listing of a Medical Device company on the Australian Stock Exchange in 2004. After the company successfully floated, she assumed the role of Chief Operations Officer. In 2006, after relocating to North America, she transitioned to Vice President of Business Development.

In 2010 Ashley started her own consulting business which led to a full time position with a Fortune 500 Company where she was responsible for the development and management of a national business initiative. After spending a significant amount of time on the road, Ashley accepted a new position in Dallas, Texas to be closer to home where she lives with her husband John and stepson Nash.

Ashley left her career as the Director of Education for a leading Digital Dentistry company in June 2015 to pursue a less demanding schedule and life balance with her family and friends.

"After digging deep and recognizing the reality of chasing something that I thought would bring happiness and security in having a successful, busy career hit me right between the eyes…. My hopes and dreams had been buried…."

Ashley is now actively involved in a dynamic organization that gives women the opportunity and means to be successful, to follow their dreams and be in control of a fulfilled and happy life!

Ashley Truitt
ashleytruitt@outlook.com
Denton, Texas

15

Daily Vitamin Hope and Warrior Wounds

Dr. Jason West

When you read this chapter, you will experience the wonderment of Integrative Health Care—amazing patient stories, stories of patient outcomes, stories of hope, faith, and healing, where we help people to regain lost vision, to leave their walker behind, to abandon a wheel chair and walk for the first time in years, to cure epileptic seizures and to cure chronic health conditions and disease.

You can restore your health, emotions and relationships. These stories will make you cry with happiness, experience great joy and most of all, give you hope.

Are you still reading? Because with this knowledge comes responsibility. You are about to be filled with the desire to share this message with your family, friends and others.

People travel from all over the world, to the little town of Pocatello, Idaho for this healing experience. You are invited to participate both in this chapter and on the video blog, www.dailydosevitaminh.com, to experience the extreme highs when people who have given up hope, get their health and life back. You will experience the lowest of the lows at times, when medical treatments fail and people die. Yes, it's a double edge sword, because that is life and sometimes death is part of life's journey.

You will experience great hope and fulfillment, which brings you tears of joy, laughter and a special connection that often leads to un-ending friendships, restoration and healing. You may connect and relate to people with similar symptoms in a special way. Your paradigms on life, health, education, ideas, new information, unheard of theories and unique medical options will be challenged. You will learn something unique and fascinating.

You may experience what Dr. West feels every day. This includes: wonderment, awe, happiness, frustration, persecution, doubt, hope, be-lief, and courage. You will get so excited about what you will see that your friends and family may not believe what you tell them.

Below are comments from some of the patients coming to the clinic for the first time:

I am coming to see you before I die . . . .

Dr. West, if you don't help me, I am going to take care of the problem (suicide).

I was trapped in my own bathroom for hours, because I could not turn the bathroom door handle and pull open the door at the same time. My once strong and functioning hands had stiffened to mere useless paddles.   -Gay Rolfe

Thanks to you I can see. I was blind before, but now I can see.

I was in a wheel chair, now I am free.

I have lost hope, and now I have it back.

I had the surgery and now it's 10x worse.

• • •

Here's the beginning of the story…

I was sitting in my office chair listening intently to another tragic health-care story. The patient was telling me of her travel through the health-care world and her complicated set of symptoms. First onset, then the emotional toll, the physical toll and then the financial toll. Because she didn't fit into a specific diagnostic category, some symptoms of multiple sclerosis but not all, some symptoms of fibromyalgia but not all, she inevitably ended up in the "it's not us, it's you" medical category of it's all in your head. "Here, take this happy pill (antidepressant) and call me in a couple of months," is typically what her medical person told her. But despite seeing 11 medical specialists, no one had ever tried to listen to what happens on a normal day, what she was eating/drinking and not one doctor had tried to restore function by balancing her physiology.

Another story of mismanagement of a lost and sick soul. I couldn't help but think, "Nothing is ever going to surprise me! I have heard it all." I just wanted to tell this patient and every other one, "Yes, I can help you!" I may not cure them. I may not take away all of their infirmities, but I really believe I can improve their quality of life. Vitamin infusion therapy, detoxification, adjustments, oxidative medicine and laser specific vitamin/mineral therapy help with nearly everyone. Couple that with the basics of good food, good air, good water, put the body on a schedule and then get very laser specific on giving the body the right bio-mechanic correction, hormone balancing and working on the emotional stresses you now have and you have a recipe that helps nearly all conditions.

You see, I had just had an amazing clinical experience. The one that makes you feel like if your professional life was to stop right there, you would know that you really helped at least one person, one family and one generation. It is my goal to get at least one amazing video testimonial every day and I was on a roll.

I had a patient tell me that she had come to my office to die and not only was she alive, she was thriving! She went from death's door to enrolling in a health care program, because I had helped her. I was riding the healer's high.

I thought that after 16 years in the trenches and 10,000 new patient interviews, I had heard it all. This was not true. I am constantly surprised by what patients tell me about their experience prior to coming to the clinic.

Here are the more common responses from medical doctors to having a chronic disease or condition:

"It's all in your head."

"You just want attention."

"You need to get off the internet, because it will convince you that you have a disease that you don't have."

"Just get a job."

"Quit being a hypochondriac"

"You just need a 'happy' pill"

"You need to have an orgasm"

"Just take this Rx for life."

"Just taking a pill might make you feel better. The pill doesn't matter."

"You have a disease that we don't know about."

"If you Google this condition and find something out, please tell me."

I have amazing clinical outcomes from people with chronic conditions, and before I can tell you the recipe (7 steps), here is the story behind the story.

I was bustling down the hall with my assistant in tow. I love having a busy office and today was no different. I love being so busy that I don't have time to sit down. I just go from patient to patient until after 5 pm and then go home, rinse, dry and repeat.

My patient, Greg, stands in front of me in the hall. He puts up a great big hand like a police officer at an intersection and says, "Dr. West, stop right there." Uh oh, what happened" my mind starts asking, "what's wrong?" All of my patients are really important to me and I get really concerned when I think there is a problem.

Greg had come to the office at the recommendation of a very famous retired NBA athlete, John Stockton. Greg had been diagnosed with reactive arthritis and was put on some very powerful but very toxic immuno-modulator (translation chemotherapy) medications before coming to my office. Greg was not doing well and the retired athlete had told him to drop everything and get to my office.

Naturally, Greg was skeptical because who would live and practice in Pocatello, Idaho? Then John told him, "Greg, I can go anywhere in the world for health care and this is where I would go. Just get in the car and go there."

About a year before, Greg had limped and walked into the office as a very sick, very tired and very skeptical patient. His background was as an investigative journalist (he has 15 Emmy's) and if I had known that, I always tell Greg, I would have never let him come to the office. He couldn't move well, his stomach was horrible with severe bowel problems; his circulation was terrible, with brain fog, depression, anxiety and everything in between. During the course of the treatment, Greg got his hope and his health back and his keen investigative sense. I was in for the experience of a lifetime, and I thought I had experienced every patient interaction available in my world.

You see, Greg is one of my wonderful patient outcome "miracles". He has completely beat reactive arthritis (it was misdiagnosed). It was really chronic Lyme disease. His story on its own is miraculous.

We treated him with IV Vitamin C, ozone, lifestyle modifications (he started eating better and taking care of himself), and laser specific vitamin therapy. He was a walking billboard for tough cases.

"Dr. West, you gotta let me talk to some of the patients!" *Talk to patients, what's Greg asking now? All he does is talk to people* is what I thought; he was always social in the patient treatment areas. He said, "I have my video camera and I want your permission to interview patients on camera." Well, who wants to go to a doctor's office and be video-taped?" was the immediate thought in my mind. How are our patients going to take a great big investigative reporter (Greg is 6′6″) with a video camera going around my office?

Every once in a while, you have one of those moments when the universe stops because of a profound revelation. I was happy in my own little cocoon (in my integrative medical practice) and didn't realize all of the "miracles" that were happening on a daily basis.

You see, I expect to help everyone who receives treatment at the clinic (maybe they will not be completely cured, but I believe that we will improve our patient's health and their quality of life). Greg tells me, "I want to document the 'miracles' I see at the clinic."

I was so absorbed by patient care that I wasn't completely aware of the impact of my life's work, until Greg started walking around the office with his video camera. Here are two of the hundreds of patient testimonials and stories that are really important.

One of the greatest feelings of happiness in my life is to see the impact of working with patients on a daily basis. Sometimes we take for granted what blessing we may be having on patients and what Greg did by videotaping these patients is special. You can see the stories on the video blog.

All of the stories are important but my team wanted me to share this one with you:

Hi, this is Amanda Tomazin and this is my story.

It was 5:30 am and I was in the middle of endless seizures and struggling to breathe. I remember the feeling that I wouldn't make it through the night and was doing everything I could to stay awake to avoid never waking up again. I was laying on the couch and my mom was across from me because I couldn't be left alone. I picked up my iPad beside me and did the best I could, to write goodbye letters to everyone I loved because I didn't think I'd have a chance to speak to them again.

Three years before that, I never thought a tick bite would

almost end my life. I was a perfectly healthy 15-year-old girl.

I was playing soccer, going to school, staying active and loved to read. I'd never imagined that one morning on May 11, 2012, when I woke up in bed with a flu that it'd take three years and hundreds of thousands of dollars to recover.

I'm now 19 years old and even though I've had Lyme disease for more than 14 years, I was only diagnosed in July of 2012 after begging the doctor to sign off on an order.

When I was five years old, my family was camping out in the Ocala National Forest in Florida. During that time, I got bit by a tick and within weeks of the tick bite, I started having symptoms that would drag on for the next six years. I was having an autoimmune reaction called vitiligo where my skin turned white on many different spots on my body and then I had extreme vision loss, headaches, stomach aches, extreme joint pain to the point that I couldn't walk for weeks at a time, fainting spells, blacking out at school, memory loss, forgetfulness, numbness, shooting pain throughout my body and fatigue. The TMJ in my jaw had gotten so bad that I was unable to open my mouth for more than 10 months.

When I was about 12 years old, my symptoms started to subside some and for about a year and a half I was almost symptom-free. Of course, I had a headache here and there, my vision didn't get better, but it was no longer getting worse, and my joints would ache from time to time. I wasn't 100% but it was the best that I'd felt in years.

Then in the summer of 2010, I was 14 years old and I started working on our family farm almost every day. Feeding the animals, picking things in the field, whatever it was, I was outside almost all day every day in the tall grass. There were ticks all the time but we thought nothing of it. When I started school back up, I went from a straight A student, reading more than 50 books during the summer, not having to work very hard to do well in school, to having a very hard time doing anything. My mom noticed that I was having trouble concentrating, things were much harder to do, and I was ditzy, and not understanding things or getting jokes as quickly as I did before. I stared getting sick again.

I had strep throat three times over the course of five months. I was playing soccer for my school and I noticed that I was having a lot more trouble keeping up with the other girls doing the exercises, and just getting much more worn out than I had in years before. When soccer ended I started doing P90X and sticking with it. I was having symptoms that I should've noticed, but I just placed into the back of my mind since I did not want to get sick again. But then I woke up one morning telling my mom I just didn't feel right. I couldn't handle noise, I couldn't handle light, the headache, joint pain, vision problems, chest pain and confusion. I was unable to keep up with conversations and was sleeping 18 hours a day.

All of my symptoms were back but much, much worse than before. My mom was alarmed at the way I looked. Just overnight, I started looking so sick and frail. She took me to my doctor and they wanted to run some tests but then nothing was wrong. My symptoms got worse, I was no longer able to get out of bed I couldn't walk upstairs. I was unable to eat and I lost 30 pounds. The symptoms were scary, to say the least. Nobody had any idea what was wrong with me and I honestly thought I would die. I'd seen over 60 doctors since I was six and none of them had been able to tell me what was wrong. It got to the point that I went to my mom and requested to have all of my medical records, any blood work or tests that ever had done sent to our house so that I could look through them. Within two weeks of being able to look over every bit of my records, making charts, circling, highlighting whatever it was, I came to the conclusion that I had Lyme disease. After talking with my parents, and watching the documentary on Lyme disease "under our skin", we decided I did have Lyme disease.

Two weeks later, after begging a doctor to sign off on an order, we had a positive test result for Lyme disease. I was so relieved and I was happy to finally have an answer. However, I had no idea the troubles that we would face getting treatment. I was just looking forward to being healthy again.

I had two positive tests and all the symptoms, even a bull's-eye rash, but doctors still refused to believe that I had Lyme disease. I got to the point that I was no longer able to walk, or read. I had days that I couldn't even speak or handle any kind of light or noise and had hundreds of seizures. The Lyme disease had spread to my brain, my heart, my muscles, my bones, my organs—to every part of my body. The oxygen flow to my brain had slowed, the blood flow to my brain had slowed and a SPECT scan even confirmed that it was from the Lyme disease. Doctors told me it was all in my head, I was crazy, I was depressed, I needed to see a psychiatrist. They said anything as long as they did not have to admit that I had Lyme disease and treat me. Doctors shouldn't be scared to treat somebody with a very real condition, because they fear they'll get their license taken away. This is affecting many more people than we know. It is ruining lives. Doctors have tried telling me that I have multiple sclerosis, chronic fatigue, fibromyalgia, Lupus, arthritis, without ever having a positive test result. But then I have two positive test results for Lyme disease and they tell me I don't have it.

Three years into this illness, I'd reached my lowest point. I'd lost all of my friends. I was alone. I was sick. I'd gotten to the point that I couldn't feed myself, bathe myself, get dressed, talk at times, and couldn't even recognize my own family. Every day was a fight to survive. It was a fight that was slowly draining me. Every breath was a struggle and doctors suggested putting me on a feeding tube and leaving me in the hospital because I wouldn't get better and I truly never thought I would.

I had prepared myself to die. As hard as it was and as much as I wanted to live, fighting was too hard. I was ready to be put out of my misery. However, one day my uncle was listening to "Seasons on the Fly" and Greg was talking about The West Clinic and his treatment for Lyme disease. After he told my parents about the clinic, they immediately started researching it. My parents made the decision that my mom and I would move to Idaho and split up our family for six months in a last ditch effort to save my life.

We didn't have any options left and even though we'd spent so much money already, we finally saw a glimpse of hope. I never expected to get better or to walk again. I was extremely skeptical, but after getting to the clinic and meeting Dr. J and getting treatment every day, I slowly started feeling better and better. It was hard to believe since I'd seen improvement with other treatments, only to plateau or get sick again. However, at The West Clinic, I just kept getting better and healthier. I soon began reading and writing again, the seizures stopped, and at the end of five months, I took my first steps in two years. Two years! It's been a year since I started walking now and getting back to living a normal life. I got my GED after missing so much high school and am going on to hopefully become a physician's assistant and help others the way that Dr. J helped me.

DR. JASON WEST *is the owner of the world- renowned,West Clinic located in Pocatello, Idaho. Patients come from every U.S. state and every continent in the world. The West Clinic was started in 1916, so we will celebrate 100 years in practice this year! There have been four generations of doctors and six generations of patients.*

Dr. West provides treatments for patients who are out of hope, out of time and out of medical options. If you need a boost of Vitamin Hope please visit our blog—www.dailydoseofvitaminh.com—where we continually post some of our amazing clinical outcomes and patient stories. We routinely help people with Lyme disease, arthritis, fibromyalgia, rheumatoid arthritis, MS, and in rebuilding people's health after a serious illness (cancer, traumas and surgeries). Dr. West and the West Clinic have been featured in three health care documentaries, Doctored, Un-doctored, *and* Medical Breakthroughs. *He has also written a # 1 Amazon Best Seller,* Hidden Secrets to Curing Your Chronic Disease, *the* West Clinic Cookbook *and a book written specifically for health care providers,* 100 Practice Tips from 100 Years in Practice *and is currently writing a book for doctors called* The Destination Practice.

Dr. West has lectured all over the United States and around the world from Canada to Australia. In addition to his practice at the West Clinic, Dr. West also has a coaching and consulting program for doctors. Dr. West teaches other doctors the medical procedures, treatments and modalities developed over the 100-year history of the clinic. In addition, he teaches about clinic culture, business practices and values. Doctors who attend our seminars or join our coaching program, that incorporate our business and treatment protocols, have increased their patient base, improved patient outcomes and have increased their profitability.

For more information please go to: www.drjseminars.com

Dr. West is married to his sweetheart, Maxine and has five sons. His family loves the outdoors, snowmobiling and motorcycle riding.

Dr. West says, "Personally, I enjoy technology, computers and how they help in medicine. I love to study relationships and communication. People think it takes a lot of courage to see an alternative medical provider and sometimes it does. In today's ever changing healthcare environment, it takes a warrior to fight the status quo, the establishment, misdiagnosed patients and the standards of care. You have to have courage to be that alternative healthcare provider. I am a warrior for my patients and I have many wounds from protecting and healing our patients."

Dr. Jason West
drjasonwest@me.com
www.dailydosevitaminh.com
208-380-9107

16

Pappou, Me and the Olive Tree
Debra Zafiropoulos

Dare to be a difference maker. Who? Me???… Just the words dare, difference and maker evoke a deep seeded emotion of questionable worthiness. To me the epitome of a difference maker is the life's work of icons like Mother Theresa of Calcutta who dedicated her life to bringing light and the love of God's tender mercy to all, especially the poorest of the poor. Stephen Hawking, hailed as the smartest man in the world and the author of the most recent book I read called *A Brief History of Time* was diagnosed at 21 with ALS, a crippling motor neuron disease. He surpassed the average life expectancy and continues to write, speak and inspire. And Jethro, the stoic K9 who tugged at the world's heartstrings after being fatally shot in the line of duty while responding to a burglary call. These are difference makers, not me, or could I be?

When I reread the introductory paragraph, I reflected upon the commonality of these difference makers and I discovered that they all had passion, undeniable courage to face life's challenges and a deep seeded commitment to help others, whether it was in word or deed. I also quickly remembered that I was challenged to step out of my comfort zone with the great opportunity to be included in this volume of *Dare To Be A Difference Maker*!

I thought about all the great philosophers, scientists, humanitarians and the people who have influenced me in my life. These individuals at some time in their lives must have come to the realization that their life's work was to just to surrender to the journey. It was then I turned towards the mirror across from my desk to see my reflection and conjured up the courage to ask; do you have the capacity to surrender up? Do you have a relentless passion for something specific and is it worthy of declaring? Have you had to dig deep sometime in your life to face life's uninvited challenges? Finally, are you committed in some way, shape or form to help others?... The answer was YES!... "*Yes!*" I said out loud, which also startled me.

My name is Debra Zafiropoulos, the middle child of amazing Greek parents, little sister to George and big sister to Christina. My life was by and large very similar to the *Big Fat Greek Wedding* movie, (with some major or minor differences depending on the perspective you heard). My father Yannis, or John, was born on the island of Crete, and met my beautiful mother Maria at a Rexall drug store while the submarine he was an engineer on, was dry docked for repair for two years at the Navy Yard in Philadelphia. Back in those days, courting with a chaperone was customary yet against all odds they fell secretly and deeply in love. When the repairs were completed my dad returned to Greece, my mom quickly followed. They were married and came back to start their new life in the United States!

Nice, beautiful, love, marriage and soon a baby in the baby carriage! My brother George was first, then me and then the best birthday present I could ever ask for, my beautiful sister Christina Maria, born on my birthday exactly five years apart! I did mention that my dad was an engineer, right?

Life as a child was fantastic with not a care in the world. We went to American school, Greek school, summer school and then started it all over again with the exception of an intermittent summer vacation to Greece to visit my paternal grandparents and large numbers of ever-growing descendants.

I remember one hot summer afternoon when everyone was taking a siesta, going to the back patio of my grandparent's house to try and cool off under the shade of the grapevines that Pappou Georgios, my grandfather, proudly pruned and manicured from the rooftop terrace. To my surprise, Pappou was sitting at the table, wearing his pajamas and a fishing cap we brought him from the states. I remember seeing the joy in his smile as he waved me over as if he had a secret he wanted only me to know.

I sat next to him on the prickly, dried-out straw chair, intently leaning forward as not to miss a single word. I focused on his every word, listening to his soft voice begin to tell a story so faintly so that he would not wake anyone and miss this opportunity for our secret story time.

Pappou recounted story after story about his family, his childhood and how he did not have the opportunity to go to school, or to wear new clothes or to go on summer vacations to foreign lands like we did. His life was hard and full of endless hours of manual labor. There was very little food and yet he focused his efforts to continuously drive hard to make a better life for his family than the one he had. I marveled at his strength and love to always do the right thing in the face of plight and despair. I now know where my father gets his work ethic from.

For what seemed like a fleeting moment, every day that summer I snuck out at siesta time to meet my pappou under the grapevines. I absorbed every story, every detail and every hardship. I realized how fortunate I was to have this time with him, to embrace his wisdom and I believe he enjoyed the opportunity to giggle at my silly stories. By virtue of being Greek, my Pappou possessed the genetic predisposition or gift of philosophizing about what I considered end of the world situations as recounted by a teenage middle daughter of a first generation Greek father. Pappou effortlessly converted every impossible teenage rant into a teaching of the fundamentals of life and the expectation of fairness and equality. His gentle, yet stern demeanor resonated with the importance of courage, perseverance and integrity in all actions. Pappou taught us to believe in ourselves, protect the integrity of our family name, to be respectful of our parents and to do our best in school so that when we had families of our own we would impart the same sentiments. I admit I was young and didn't see the value of his words until much later in life.

Summer came to an end and we boarded the plane back to America to resume three cycles of America school, Greek school and summer school before we returned to Greece again. I was thrilled. I couldn't wait to see my family and experience another summer in my beloved Greece!

That summer was dramatically different. Everyone was older including my aunts, uncles, cousins and especially my grandparents. The neighborhood looked smaller and the energy wasn't as light and joyous as I experienced in summers past. I immediately noticed Pappou's perfectly manicured grapevines were dry, disheveled and barren of fruit.

The first siesta was taken to get over jet lag and also the next one. By the third day, I silently retreated to the patio where the same prickly, dried-out straw chair sat waiting for me, as did my Pappou. He was dressed in his pajamas and he still had the old fishing cap from summers past. He loved that cap, it was now just a bit more faded. I saw my Pappou as my hero, gentle yet still stoic. Pappou was older, slower and without his intention, the joy in his smile that I remembered was replaced with a blank somewhat distant gaze. I wasn't prepared for that. I remember trying to engage in conversation with him, bringing up stories we shared from previous summers, but it was to no avail. I remembered that he loved when my sister and I massaged lotion onto his hands and feet and now his once strong hands were frail and crooked. What used to result in a bright smile and deep seeded laughter had no effect at all. Why? What wasn't I doing right?

I didn't know then what I know now. "Pappou is just 'forgetful'," everyone said as if that was ok. Today it would be termed dementia or Alzheimer's. This was the first summer I had to take a siesta instead of sitting under the vines with Pappou. I tossed and turned the summer away playing his words and countless stories in my head so as not to forget. I remembered a particular story about trees—olive trees specifically. Pappou asked me what I thought the purpose of the olive tree was... *Purpose,* I thought? Well to make oil for cooking french fries and olives for our salad I replied. Chuckling, he responded, "Bravo, but the olive tree has no purpose until someone needs something from it. Olive trees have been around for thousands and thousands of years and it is perfectly content being a tree," he continues. "It only has a purpose if an animal needs shelter from the elements or someone is hungry and needs the fruit from its branches. Otherwise the olive tree is just an olive tree, perfectly happy and content with just being an olive tree." I tried to see the message in the story and what I realized is that just like the olive tree we have no purpose in life but to just be; be happy and content. I realize that my grandfather was just like the olive tree, even in his current state—perfectly happy and content. It was I who needed him to be more. I immediately learned one of my most precious lessons: I just have to be happy and content within myself, I do not have to do anything, just be me and those around me will find what they need. It's like love: love is not what you do, love is what you are and when you are love, it's shelter, it's nourishment, it is magic.

That summer, we spent quality time with my grandparents and made the best of times even in his silence. As we prepared to leave that summer, I could feel the heaviness in the air and the painful thought that we might never see Pappou again. The morning we were to depart, we woke hearing my grandmother calling after my Pappou in Greek, "Georgios! Georgios! Where are you going?" He responded, "To the Barber to get a shave before we have to go to the airport!" Somehow, someway, he came back to us!

I quickly ran to his side and out the door we went to the barbershop up the street, hand in hand, with his ever-present fishing cap and cane—off we went just like the good old days. His eyes twinkled as we shuffled in the morning sunshine. I could never put into words how elated and emotional I felt that day. We all had a gleaming hope in our hearts that the Pappou we enjoyed so much had come back to us, if by the miracle of our prayers. Unfortunately by the time we said our goodbyes at the terminal, the same distant gaze had returned on my beloved Pappou's clean-shaven face. Why? What happened? Where did he go?

"Pappou! Pappou!" I cried on his shoulder, as I had to let go to board the plane. "Why did this happen?" I cried. My mom softly responded, "I don't know." That was our last visit with Pappou; he passed shortly after. Through all our sadness, I was resolved to never ever forget what we shared and the lessons that would serve as the foundation to my essence and integrity.

I realize now that what I learned from all my grandparents' and my parents' life experiences was not intended to be used as emotional black-mail into staying on the right path, but as an opportunity to see that life has as many obstacles as opportunities and it is the emotion behind the decision or action that could make the outcome either monumental or tragic.

Fast forward—I graduated college and entered the dental profession, and the quest for knowing the 'why' behind disease origins came back. I recall treating patients early in my career removing shards and shards of calculus (tartar) buildup and hearing patient after patient thank me for doing a great job "cleaning their teeth". I began to wonder if I had made the worst decision of my life by choosing dentistry. Was I reduced to being a cleaning lady licensed specifically to the oral cavity? Why didn't my patients appreciate that I worked hard at getting a formal education and that I had a passion for caring for people and I did more that just clean teeth! I remembered the story of the olive tree and that I was not happy or content with my current state of employment. I knew I had to either change my outlook or the passion for dental medicine and caring for patients would be reduced to doing a job and collecting a paycheck, and that wasn't in my DNA.

Then, it happened. One day while doing a preliminary oral tissue exam, I felt a small lump the size of a lima bean underneath the patients tongue. When I asked if he knew about it, he said, "Yes" and that a doctor told him it was a blocked salivary duct. He was told not to worry about it, take the antibiotics and it would go away. I asked him how long it was there and he said, "Months, and now it's beginning to bother me when I swallow." Instantly, my gut started to churn. I continued asking questions and was not pleased with any of his answers. Our office referred the patient out for a consultation with a different specialist.

A few weeks later, I saw that this patient was on my schedule. I was excited to see him and find out how he was feeling until our eyes met and the same gut wrenching feeling returned. His eyes had the same fading stare of my beloved Pappou. Ugh, I will never forget that look. I escorted him and his wife to my operatory and closed the door as he requested. As I do with all my patients, I sat down to talk with them: eye to eye, face to face. Immediately, he reached out to my hand and softly said "Thank You. My wife and I want to thank you for taking such good care of me. You offered more compassion and diligence by not letting the spot under my tongue fester without knowing what it really was." With that, he told me that he had a biopsy, followed by a PET scan that resulted in the diagnosis of stage IV oral and pharyngeal cancer. For the first time ever in my life, I experienced what it was like to go into shock. As with any moment the word 'Cancer' is spoken, the rest of the appointment was a blur. The only memory from that moment was the complete and utter feeling of helplessness and that blasted word with endless non-descript resolutions; Why? Why bounced across my brain like a frantic ping-pong ball! Why did this happen? Why wasn't this diagnosed earlier? I never wanted to be in that situation again. I set out to make sure I wouldn't be.

I now had a bigger purpose than being known as a great dental hygienist! I wanted to save people from the 'C' word and make a difference in my patient's lives! It was then I made my declaration…I would never allow a spot to walk out of my operatory without knowing what it was! I devoted every waking hour researching all that I could about the 'C' word, all types of cancer, epithelial and oral cancer, throat cancer to HPV related cancer. I searched for the best and most current scientifically sound clinical reports, cutting edge screening methods and treatments to educate myself.

Not being a formally trained dentist or physician did not sway me. I quickly earned the respect of my peers and began creating programs and presenting them all over the country. While I grew my knowledge base and confidence, the proverbial question of 'Why' patients were being diagnosed late stage with cancer kept resurfacing. I quickly saw a missing piece of the puzzle. As a result I changed direction and studied prevention. This included all forms of prevention from tactile exams, technology, salivary diagnostics and communication. I studied anything that I could get my hands on, spoke with anyone who would answer my calls, and visited many prestigious cancer facilities in search of information and to build valuable relationships. With great support and genuine mentorship, I converted my programs into more proactive cancer prevention training that provided the attendees with a plan of action in prevention, screening, communication and the confidence to screen to save lives!

In 2015 I founded NationalCancerNetwork.org a 501(c)(3) after losing a dear friend to secondary cancer which was finally located on her tongue after being in remission from triple negative breast cancer. The National Cancer Network is growing our worldwide team that is laser focused and determined to meet our vision of a world free of cancer. Our mission is to raise awareness to prevent late stage diagnosis of cancer through multiple platforms of prevention, progress in science and technology, screening events and referral protocols.

This hit home personally for me this year as I found a small spot on my forehead and when it did not go away in two weeks, I followed the same protocol I teach in my programs and had it examined. It took three different consultations until one dermatologist said she would take a biopsy as I requested whereas the others just wanted to "watch it." She reassured me that it didn't look bad and not to worry, it was probably nothing. With my training I knew that any visual exam and tactile exam was not a diagnosis and waited for the pathology report, plus my gut radar was on red alert. A few days later to the surprise of my physician and me I was diagnosed with skin cancer and was immediately scheduled for surgery and the MOHS procedure. The surgeon told me that if it was not diagnosed at this stage that within 3-4 years it would have taken over at minimum the top right quarter of my forehead or more. I submit the moral to this experience is to stick to your gut, if you are not getting the answers to your questions, keep searching.

I feel fortunate to have had the tender moments with my Pappou Georgios and my YiaYia Sophia. My maternal grandparents in the states Pappou Haralambos, my beloved namesake YiaYia Despina, my godmother Christine Leonard, my family, numerous friends and mentors who all saw in me what took me this assignment to acknowledge. This writing experience reminded me that when I am happiest and content with me, those around me are even happier. It instilled in me the confidence to continue to feed my passion, to be a leader who inspires change in the world and to share the gifts of life's treasures to all of those around me by just being.

Today, I am proud to be and active part in the movement to make cancer history. I credit the difference makers like Mother Theresa and others in our midst that remain like the olive tree, content and happy with just being an olive tree or whatever it needs to be without expectations.

I thank you for taking your time to learn about me and I hope you look at your mirror and ask; Do you have a relentless passion for something specific and is it worthy of declaring? I know you do! Dare To Be A Difference Maker!

DEBRA ZAFIROPOULOS *or Debbie Z, as she is lovingly called, is the founder of the OralED Institute, a division of Delta Force Group Consulting which is a collaborative firm that leads you from Current State to Desired State. Whether it is taking science and technology off the shelf and into implementation for clients to provide optimal long-term health therapies for patients while improving their bottom line or mastering the responsibilities of leadership and management or achieving personal excellence in sales or culture, Delta Force has the knowledge, systems processes and tools to get you to your goal.*

Debbie is a tireless pioneer health crusader, educator and author dedicated to Total Health Initiatives and Making Oral Cancer History. This passion drove Debbie to form NationalCancerNetwork.org a 501(C) (3), whose vision is to raise awareness of prevention, progress, screening and referrals for a vision of a cancer free world. Although in its infancy, the support from consumers and professionals has been overwhelming. With Debra's passion and assembly of like-minded humanitarians, there is no doubt that together they will catapult the NationalCancerNetwork.org into a highly effective and charitable organization.

"Delay is the enemy of action, Fear stagnates action and neither exist in a hero's heart, eliminate both and your heart is open to your super hero!" – Debbie Zafiropoulos

Debbie is fiercely committed to delivering powerful messages to communities worldwide on personalized systems so they can define goals, focus activities and finally live the business and personal life of their dreams. If you are looking for a dynamic speaker and proven professional who can guide you out of chaos and into productivity, then you have come to the right place.

With over 27 years in the health industry and working with a variety of clients, Debbie's laser focus and ability to get to the cause holding you back guiding you to achieve remarkable success. My mission and commitment to you is to ignite the hero within you!

debbiez@debbiezrdh.com
Learn about the non-profit at: WWW.NationalCancerNetwork.org
DebbieZ@NationalCancerNetwork.org
561-358-7660